16, 22

The Scope of Planning Required.
P. 64   Housing

Urban Planning in the Developing Countries

PRAEGER SPECIAL STUDIES IN
INTERNATIONAL ECONOMICS AND DEVELOPMENT

Urban Planning in the Developing Countries

Edited by
John D. Herbert
and
Alfred P. Van Huyck

Published in cooperation with
Planning and Development Collaborative International

FREDERICK A. PRAEGER, Publishers
New York · Washington · London

The purpose of the Praeger Special Studies is to make specialized research monographs in U.S. and international economics and politics available to the academic, business, and government communities. For further information, write to the Special Projects Division, Frederick A. Praeger, Publishers, 111 Fourth Avenue, New York, N.Y. 10003.

FREDERICK A. PRAEGER, PUBLISHERS
111 Fourth Avenue, New York, N.Y. 10003, U.S.A.
5 Cromwell Place, London S.W. 7, England

Published in the United States of America in 1968
by Frederick A. Praeger, Inc., Publishers

© 1968 by Frederick A. Praeger, Inc.

Library of Congress Catalog Card Number: 68-18917

Printed in the United States of America

PREFACE

The material included in this book was first presented at a seminar held in Washington, D.C., on July 28, 1967. This meeting was sponsored by the Planning and Development Collaborative International (PADCO, Inc.) in conjunction with its Annual General Meeting.

PADCO is an international collaborative formed by experts in the planning and development fields and owned by a diversified group of professionals from firms and universities around the world. Its main purpose is to provide governments and private clients in Africa, Asia, Latin America, and the Near East with integrated research, planning, and management services for urban and regional development. These services include planning for the renewal and expansion of established cities, the development of new centers of urbanization, the development of the regional transportation and communication networks on which urbanization depends, urban and regional administration, and the financing of urban development. Secondary services are offered in fields of concern where planning must be linked closely with urbanization. These include natural resource development, agriculture, and the development of rural community facilities.

PADCO, as a matter of policy, presents an annual series of papers concerning planning in the developing countries at a private seminar. The annual seminar reflects the group's interest in supporting urban planning in a variety of ways--through direct consultation, through research, through training, and through organized exchanges of knowledge among scholars and practitioners.

The 1967 Seminar was concerned with the immense urban implementation task facing the developing areas. The seminar group examined the relevance of present planning methods and advanced a series of suggestions for the improvement of work in and for the developing areas. All of the papers presented at the seminar were given by members of the PADCO Board of Directors.

In 1968, the subject will be "National Policies for Urbanization." Discussions will be focused on the need for stronger urban programs at the national

level and on steps that can be taken to link urban
planning more exactly with the basic economics of
social planning.

In preparing this series of papers for publica-
tion, the editors wish to acknowledge the effort of
Miss Margie Starkey, who typed the manuscript and
successfully coped with the format details.

CONTENTS

LIST OF TABLES AND GRAPHS

TABLES

GRAPHS

INTRODUCTION

The seminar on which the chapters in this volume are based was concerned with one of the most important, troublesome, and, at the same time, promising characteristics of the twentieth century--urbanization in the developing countries. The changes accompanying rapid urbanization bring with them vast population shifts, the need for rapid technological advance, radical changes in values and customs, and, in many cases, major changes in administrative systems. If the challenge posed by such changes is to be met, the developing nations must utilize fully their present skills and talents. They will, no doubt, have to continue to borrow techniques from the developed areas. But it is becoming increasingly clear that many of those techniques are not appropriate for the kinds of change that must be achieved.

Urban development is a fundamental part of, and key to, over-all economic and social development.

Robert B. Mitchell, in the first chapter of this study, emphasizes the importance of linking urban policy more effectively with national economic planning and establishes a base for the discussions developed in each of the other chapters. Mitchell reviews the characteristics of the developing areas that are relevant for urban planning. He points out important variations within specific developing areas--including, among others, differences in concern with the public interest and private rights, differences in degrees of public participation in the economy, marked differences in income and employment levels, differences in social structure, differences even in the nature of migration from rural to urban areas, and differences in the extent to which usable urban capital is already established. He also reviews the major similarities in urbanization problems that developing areas face and emphasizes the need to develop fresh techniques for dealing with rapid and complex growth. These new approaches would depend largely on existing data and would bypass unnecessarily sophisticated techniques currently used in the developed areas--a point to which John D. Herbert's chapter is addressed. In discussing the common concern with renewal in the major centers of developing areas, he warns against the types of massive clearance programs that have been used in the United States. Alfred P. Van Huyck carries this

point further in Chapter 4, discussing work done
recently in India. Mitchell concludes discussion
of this topic with an analysis of the need to
develop substantially new approaches to planning,
with emphasis on the development of effective
planning processes rather than on the type of static
planning typical of the past.

In Chapter 2, Herbert bases his suggestions for
the type of planning process that he believes likely
to be effective on metropolitan planning in the
developing areas. Emphasizing the important role
that major urban centers already play in developing
countries, he argues that the scope of urban planning
that is addressed to these centers must be much
broader than the typical scope of "city planning"
in the West. He recognizes the general scarcity of
data that characterizes the developing areas and the
value that can be gained from using seasoned judgments of people familiar with particular localities,
then goes on to discuss the types of analytical tools
that are needed to deal systematically with the most
urgent issues. He describes the characteristics of
tools that now are being developed and on which he
has already done some preparatory work, tools
designed specifically to make it possible to break
down very complex policy problems into manageable
subproblems and to identify sequences in which the
subproblems can be attacked efficiently. These
tools are used also to predict the likely impacts
of alternative policies that may be implemented.
Help in identifying strategic entry points in
metropolitan systems--entry points at which particular governmental and private actions are likely to
be most effective--is a further possible result of
refined analytic tools. They could also allow
traditional statistical data and the qualitative
judgments of informed practitioners and policy-makers
to be combined in the same framework. Herbert
re-emphasizes the points made by Mitchell and
stresses the importance of developing adequate
planning machinery. He urges that planning be
carried on at several levels simultaneously--dealing
with both immediate and long-run issues. He
emphasizes the importance of developing effective
systems for acquiring and processing the data that
are needed most urgently for urban policy. Such
systems should be developed gradually, he feels,
and premature accumulations of data that have been
associated with computerization in the United
States and elsewhere should be avoided. He is

concerned also with a point developed more fully in
the fifth chapter--the importance of strengthening
both administration and planning and the necessity
of preparing a variety of professional skills for
planning and implementation, rather than focusing
on planning alone.

In Chapter 3, Masahiko Honjo addresses himself
to the problem of administrative development for
planning and reveals in a major case study the
"growing pains" that national and local administrations are likely to experience in the process of
developing effective urban administrative systems.
He traces the history of administrative development
in Japan, which was not unlike that in the United
States and may presage the types of evolution that
are likely to occur in a number of developing areas.
Evidence of such development is visible already in
both Latin America and Asia. The lessons to be
learned from Japan should prove very useful to other
developing areas.

In Chapter 4, Van Huyck relates a number of the
points made in the three preceding chapters to the
specific problem of housing in India. He stresses
the importance of attacking the housing problems of
developing areas in the context established by
over-all plans. In the past, housing has often
been approached from a humane but economically and
administratively narrow view, which has led to
proposals that could not be implemented. Van Huyck
re-emphasizes the importance of developing new
planning concepts and new approaches to the entire
concept of "housing." He argues that housing policy
must be linked directly with existing market processes
and that it must recognize the limits of present
governmental capacities for implementation. The
project he discusses and the approaches taken elsewhere in India, with which he compares it, are
suggestive of fresh types of housing policy that are
likely to be effective in many parts of the world.

William L. C. Wheaton's concluding chapter
concentrates on training, one of the most important
parts of the logistic support required for effective
planning. Reflecting the points raised in Mitchell's
and Herbert's chapters, he underscores the immediate
need for planning that is consistent with the broad
economic, social, administrative, and environmental
factors now present in most low-income countries of
the world. Wheaton believes that implementing

agencies must receive a large part of the attention directed at improving the quality of development. Within the field of "planning" itself, a wide variety of planning skills should be developed, composed primarily of specialists and relatively few generalists. This planning structure would require types of training markedly different from the types of generalist training now provided in the United States and Europe, and Wheaton urges that training capacities in the developing countries themselves be used--capitalizing on the developing areas' sensitivity to their own training needs. Complementing this proposal, he asks for more imaginative participation within the developing areas by experts and institutions from the developed countries. The perennial problem of the "brain drain," in which some of the best talents of developing areas are drawn to more lucrative and professionally rewarding work in developed areas, is at the heart of Wheaton's analysis. His imaginative suggestions for dealing with this problem deserve to be developed fully and tested in a combined effort by both the developed and developing areas.

Urban Planning in the
Developing Countries

CHAPTER **1** URBAN DEVELOPMENT
PROBLEMS AND
OPPORTUNITIES

Robert B. Mitchell*

The rapid urban development occurring all over
the world is not always an effect of the same forces,
but it must be considered a part of world-wide
economic and social development. During the last
few years, an increasing number of papers presented
at international development meetings have repeated
what should be two well-known truths: first, that
economic development implies social and cultural
change and that social development planning should
accompany economic development planning; second, that
economic development planning is too often blind to
the space dimension and that the areal distribution
of economic activities is a necessary element of
economic planning. Development experts propose
economic development plans for region and area, as
well as for sector.

Although all nations are "developing" nations,
they are developing in different manners, within
different rules, with different resources, and at
different rates. They are starting from different
levels of development and different degrees of
complexity in their economic and social organization,
roughly called the "three worlds of development" by

_____

*Robert B. Mitchell, B.A., is Chairman of the
Board of PADCO, Inc., Planning and Development
Collaborative International, and Chairman of the
Department of City and Regional Planning at the
University of Pennsylvania.

the sociologist Irving Louis Horowitz. His three
worlds are described as: a) the United States and
Western Europe, which have developed within the
individualist, competitive, capitalist, parliamentary
tradition; b) the Soviet Union and its satellites,
which emphasize state central direction, central
planning, and socialism; and c) the "third world,"
which is comprised of those nations outside the first
two blocs that are conscious of an urgent need for
economic and social development but do not find in
either of the first two worlds a clear pattern they
wish to follow. Horowitz also mentions a "fourth
world" of the tribal societies, which, for one reason
or another, are not aware of alternatives to their
ways of life. He points out that the "third world"
nations differ vastly in history, social and cultural
tradition, political system, and stage of economic
and technical development.

In all three worlds, the present nature and
condition of cities is largely a function of the
economic and social development of their nations,
but affected in many instances by a city's historic
role in the colonial system of the past.

If there is this close relationship between both
the nature and role of urban places and the development
process of a country, it would seem apparent that:
a) each economic and social development plan should
include a strategy of urbanization, and b) urban
plans must be process-oriented and firmly based on
the planned processes of economic and social
development.

Ideally, a strategy of urbanization includes a
plan and a proposed method of implementation. It has
a plan for the location, size, function, and growth
rate of settlements in a region or nation. In a
region such as "Appalachia," it conceivably could
provide for the reduction in size or change in
function of some settlements. Such a plan, stating
a desired urbanization pattern, needs to be
accompanied by a program for diverse public actions,
including investments intended to guide and control
the urbanization process.

Thus, urbanization planning would become one
aspect of economic development planning with a space
dimension, based on research into the economic and
social consequences of alternative distributions of
settlement--and including policies for the relative
concentration or dispersion of population and
economic activities.

All three of the so-called worlds of development
can furnish examples of planning for the distribution
of urban settlements that is closely tied to the
desired distribution of jobs in a region or nation.
The drive of the Soviet Union to establish industrial
complexes and new cities, particularly east of the
Urals, is well known. Israel has adopted policies
favoring the development of certain regions for
economic or strategic reasons and has sponsored the
establishment of new towns and villages according to
this central policy. Venezuela, concerned with the
rapid growth of the Caracas area and the industrial
towns immediately to the west, has attempted to
encourage the development of the Guayana region both
to make the most of the natural resources of that area
and to create a new pole of development that might
slow down the overwhelming growth of Caracas. Great
Britain has embarked upon regional planning programs,
has adopted policies for location of industries, and
has planned for new towns and cities in an attempt
to channel the great growth of the Southeast and to
improve the economic balance by growth in other parts
of the country. France has adopted a program of
regional development, encouraging growth around
existing provincial cities as poles of development
tied to specific national functions. East Pakistan,
faced with an overwhelming change from an agricultural
to an industrial economy and with concomitant urbanization of millions of rural people, has obtained aid from
the United Nations in planning for an urbanization
strategy of the kind described.

The United States very much needs a strategy of
urbanization, particularly for the northeast industrial
quarter of the country. Its attempts toward an urban
policy have concentrated on proposals to overcome the
urban manifestations of imbalances or inequities in
largely unplanned social and economic development.

An important part of an urbanization strategy,
in addition to locational planning, is the development
of a coherent set of national policies for the
amelioration of present social, economic, and physical
urban problems and conscious allocation of national
resources for these purposes. The so-called Model
Cities Program in the United States is a beginning
in this direction.

There are great differences in the nature,
problems, and growth rate of urban places among the
various countries. The nature of planning and
governmental organization and action are also as

varied.   In planning for urban development, these
differences require fresh and sensitive approaches.
Some reasons for these differences are as follows:

a)   If one can imagine a continuum between
extremes of emphasis on "the public interest" or on
"private rights," one finds various countries
expressing their own balances between these extremes
in their traditions and governmental policies.   The
difficulty of striking such a balance between public
and private rights is an old problem to practitioners
of the law and is recognized as a basic dilemma in
North American planning.   Closely associated with
this question is the power of government to act and
the degree of parliamentary or court control over
public policies and acts.   Probably the carefully
planned and controlled suburban expansions of
Stockholm, which raise the lowest level of environmental quality far above that found in United States
cities, also reduce the area of choice of style of
life for many people.   The paternalistic planning of
residential areas in Moscow puts much greater
emphasis on public amenities than on private amenities.

b)   Obvious causes of differences in urbanization
among countries include (1) differences in the mix of
public-private activity in the economy and (2) the
degree of dispersion of developmental decisions.   In
the Stockholm developments, most of the new residential
building is by government or by cooperative societies.
In the United States, much of the chaotic development
of suburbs, although providing a very broad choice of
style of life to people, has not really been controlled
thus far because of unwillingness to interfere with
private initiative in the production of housing.

c)   Levels of personal and household income and
the degree of unemployment or underemployment among
the labor force differ greatly.   In many countries,
a large part of the population is not really partici-
pating in the twentieth century economy or social
system.   If many Indian workers find it impossible to
pay the cost of public transportation to and from work,
this is an obvious influence on urban planning
decisions.   The importance of a substantial middle
class with the education, skills, and purchasing power
to feed a growing economy and lift living aspirations
and standards is acknowledged everywhere.   In a
number of countries, such a class is developing quite
rapidly--buying automobiles and compounding the
transportation problem.

d)   The complexity and degree of role differentiation in the social structure and economy is a less
obvious but strong influence in urban organization.
India's well-known traditional and inherited pattern
of occupations according to caste is an example of
this. At another extreme, the twentieth century
development in the process and institutions of
marketing in the United States has caused great
differences in the land use pattern of cities and
greatly increased the scale of urban texture.

e)   The extent and nature of rural to urban
migration are very important in urban development.
The shack-towns on the hills of most South American
cities house thousands of hopeful migrants who have
not been assimilated into the social or economic
structure of the city. This problem is shared by
the United States with its Negro ghettoes in all of
the major cities. Related to the problem of rural to
urban migration is the mix of ethnic or cultural
groups in the population. In Singapore, tense intergroup relations between the Malays and the Chinese,
and the dominance of Chinese in the government, have
given rise to complaints by the Malays, whether or
not warranted, that they have been discriminated
against in housing and other governmental programs.

f)   Cultural factors and expectations of the
people differ widely among parts of the world. An
example might be the varying requirements for privacy
or gregariousness which produce differentiation
between private and public life. People in Asia
seem to have less concern about privacy within the
family than people in North America. Slums in
Singapore provide little private accommodation in
housing but have a rich street life that so far has
not been transmitted to the new high-density
apartment developments or the new towns being built.

g)   The extent of accumulated urban capital in
infrastructure and buildings that are usable in the
future is an important consideration. If a city has
to provide almost completely new sanitary water supply
and sewerage systems, this can make a vast difference
in the allocation of developmental resources.

Of course, there are many other factors that
influence differences in planning for urbanization
in various parts of the world. Despite these
differences, there are many similarities from

country to country in subjects of concern in urban
development, in approach to them, and in appropriate
planning method. Let us mention a few:

a)   Large metropolitan areas are growing rapidly
in many countries. All are faced with the usual
locational planning questions about distribution and
density of population and jobs, about policies
regarding centralization or dispersion: whether to
provide for a thickening in the development of present
areas, or for their indefinite expansion, or for new
poles of development. Obviously, these questions
bring their concomitant transportation issues. In
the United States, federal agencies in transportation
and housing and most state and metropolitan planning
agencies have learned the hard way that transportation
planning is intimately bound up with this question of
population and job distribution and that alternative
patterns need evaluation. There seems to be a growing
tendency in some large cities outside of the United
States to try to adapt North American techniques of
traffic estimation and transportation planning. This
may result in costly exercises of mathematical futility,
because the studies often are not based upon an
accompanying study of land use alternatives or
realistic appraisal of future land use possibilities.
I have seen certain instances in South America which
I was told were being financed by United States
assistance. Certainly, in every city there are
examples of obvious transportation improvements
designed to meet present problems. They do not
require elaborate study. But the design of entirely
new systems of freeways or rapid transit must be tied
in with an adequate land use study and, I suspect,
should use shortcuts employing a synthesis of origin
and destination patterns and bypassing some of the
costly data collection that is being undertaken.

b)   Transportation is a recognized major problem
in most large cities around the world. When Doxiadis
was engaged in his regional plan for Rio, he remarked
that it was impossible in that city to solve the
housing problem without bringing transportation into
the solution so that areas outside the present
urbanized area could be opened up. The new settlement
of workers' houses constructed outside of Karachi
makes transportation to jobs too difficult and too
costly. An adequate transportation system can widen
job opportunities for poor people. However, most
cities find that there are grave problems in imposing
a new rapid transit or highway system on an old city.

This is exacerbated as more and more people do not
use or need public transportation because they drive
their own automobiles.

c) Many cities are concerned about deciding
whether to adapt old congested centers to new
functional requirements or to create new centers.
In a number of instances, central functions are being
dispersed, as in Honolulu where the Ala Moana Center
(a new modern construction with adequate parking) has
attracted much of the trade from the old central
business district about a half mile away. Other
central functions seem to be dispersing in a random
fashion in the general direction of Waikiki. In
Honolulu, this requires special study and development
of policies for concentration or recentralization of
central functions, closely related to transportation
solutions. A similar situation exists in Singapore,
where planners are concerned about the movement of a
number of central functions, including hotels and
office buildings, up Orchard Road, away from the
old central district. They recognize the need for
a thorough study of central district functions and
space requirements in connection with an urban
renewal program. A new major center is being planned
for the outskirts of Copenhagen, to be constructed
under private auspices. According to the plans, it
will be so large that it may largely stop the growth
of the old center and be a major factor in shaping
the future development of the Copenhagen region.
Of course, the growth of subsidiary business districts
outside the Ginza in Tokyo, related to the suburban
railroad stations, is well known.

Often, as in a number of cities in Italy, there
is concern for the preservation of historic areas or
architectural treasures in the old centers. This
generally shared sense of the importance of cultural
continuity often conflicts with new functional
requirements.

d) As mentioned previously, many cities are
faced with the problem of assimilating large in-migrant
populations of poor people, untrained in the requirements of new industrial occupations and unaccustomed
to urban ways of life--a problem common to New York
and Caracas and cities of Israel and India. In
New York, inadequate opportunity for these people to
improve their way of life is taken as a major failure
in the present functioning of the city. An important

part of contemporary comprehensive planning in New York is devoted to combining efforts in housing, education, job provision, and social and health services.

e) Many cities are concerned with undertaking urban renewal programs. The primary drive of this movement, as in early days of urban renewal in the United States, is the replacement of old, worn out, or functionally obsolete facilities by new construction. In many cities, however, including New York and Calcutta, planners are recognizing the need to conserve the housing stock, however poor, as shelter for many people. Even in the United States, resources are not sufficient to improve the quality of housing for a large sector of the population of the next generation. Tearing down housing in urban renewal programs can have a disastrous effect in actually reducing housing availability to the lowest-income families. The rate at which old housing can be torn down and replaced needs careful study, as evidenced in both Singapore and New York. Analysis of the problems of social and economic organization and cultural patterns of living is also vital to any urban renewal program.

f) Interest in building new housing communities and new towns is prevalent everywhere. One example is the vast number of new towns and small town expansions in the Soviet Union since the last war. Hong Kong and Singapore are well known for their large-scale building of housing for relatively low-income people at extremely high density. Some officials are beginning to be concerned with the possible social or political implications of these very large concentrations of low-income families at high density. And most new towns, even in the United States, have not faced the problem of building extensive new quarters for the lowest-income groups-- an absolute necessity if economic integration is to be realized.

g) Protection of health through adequate water supply and sewerage is a universal problem. Faced with an expected very large increase in metropolitan population, a high official in Bogota recently said that he believed water supply, sanitation, and transportation, in that order, would be the most pressing problems.

h) A world-wide problem is the need to discover the most effective ways by which government can

intervene to improve social and health conditions in
poverty areas. Community development experience in
rural areas in developing countries is worth
intensive study, and the United States is experiment-
ing with local organization for a measure of self-
determination in planning "antipoverty" programs.
Both intragroup and intergroup communication seem
to break down in some of these areas. Research and
a high degree of skill are needed if intervention
is to be successful.

    i) In most places, government as a whole is
poorly organized to guide or direct development in
urban areas. Social, economic, and physical aspects
of urban problems need comprehensive treatment, which
seems impossible in many places because of divided
jurisdictions in governmental agencies. Similarly,
the divided responsibilities of national, regional,
and local governmental agencies complicate the
problem. A few years ago, a special United Nations
mission in Singapore recommended a radical reallocation
of governmental powers to concentrate responsibility
for development planning and execution. This was
done and a great amount has been accomplished. In
many places, we need to invent new governmental
actions as incentives or controls to private development, and to invent new mixes of public-private
initiative and capital. In some areas, we need
to create or change a building industry or a
development financing industry. Even in New York,
there is a lack of a building industry competent to
undertake the rehabilitation of slum buildings on a
large scale.

    j) In many parts of the world, most urban
development is undertaken by government initiative.
However, cities are still relying on old-fashioned,
static plans calling for police power controls over
private development. There is a world-wide movement
toward a new kind of planning to guide developmental
processes: by setting policies and developmental
strategies and programing governmental actions,
including the allocation of investments. The new,
comprehensive planning approach in New York includes
social, economic, and physical development and is
establishing not only an over-all development strategy
for the city but also local strategies in the various
subcommunities. The planning agency and the budget
agency are working very closely together with joint
staff task forces and are considering developmental
and service programs, and matching operating to capital
budgets, as well as longer-range investment programs.

k) This new kind of strategic planning for urbanization demands that each country and metropolitan area must develop a continuing planning capability. This requires the training, partly in-service, of planning and development personnel. It means that an urban area can no longer buy a plan from a foreign consultant, but must participate in the making of that plan and must be able to carry on its refinement and adaptation as progress is made.

CHAPTER **2** AN APPROACH TO
METROPOLITAN
PLANNING IN THE
DEVELOPING COUNTRIES

John D. Herbert*

INTRODUCTION

Metropolitan planning, occurring in many
contexts, takes many forms. The developing countries
are the context for the present discussion--countries
that differ from one another considerably but have a
number of critical characteristics in common,
including relatively low per capita gross products--
generally $650 or less annually. Though one or two
have levels as high as $800 per capita per year, a
substantial proportion are at levels of less than
$200. Most of them have relatively low literacy
levels, relatively low degrees of urbanization, urban
administrative systems whose capacities are far below
those required for the gigantic development tasks
they face, and relatively unstable political systems.

Most of these countries have high population
growth rates, between 2 per cent and 3.5 per cent per
year, and per capita gross output growth rates ranging
from negative figures to 2 per cent per year, with
three or four at or near 3 per cent--compared with
rates ranging from about 3 per cent to over 9 per cent
for the relatively developed countries.

---

*John D. Herbert, B.A., Ph.D., is Vice President
for Programing and Evaluation of PADCO, Inc. He
formerly served with The Ford Foundation Planning
Advisory Group in Calcutta, India, and on the faculty
of the University of California at Berkeley.

In some instances, abundant resource bases are scarcely utilized because of inadequate organization, low labor productivity, and capital scarcities. In several areas, a more efficient use of resources and the gaining of full benefits from the comparative advantages of each country require regional alliances through the creation of common markets or analogous institutions.

In almost all cases, there is a desperate need to increase productivity more quickly and raise per capita output through concentrating on those activities in which absolute levels of output and potential growth rates offer the most hope of achieving adequate over-all growth rates. It is essential to achieve, domestically or through imports, more rapid capital accumulation and improved consumption patterns. At least in the short run, it is important to concentrate domestic production in those sectors that produce the most needed capital equipment or contribute most to improving consumption patterns, together with the competitive export sectors that can provide the foreign exchange required for essential imports. For many developing countries, this suggests, among other things, a concentration on manufacturing industries which at the moment are concentrated chiefly in the major metropolitan areas.

Coupled with this need for a concentration of effort in urban centers, there are a number of factors that induce urbanization and place severe pressures on existing centers--though the urbanization that results from them is largely statistical rather than a true technological and cultural urbanization. Rapid population growth and low productivity in the rural areas, coupled with relatively high wage rates in the cities, induce massive and persistent rural to urban migration. The reservoirs of rural population from which the pressures come are in some cases immense. In India, for example, the rural population is in the vicinity of 400 million. Many of these migrants come with the hope, rather than the reality, of a job--simply because the mother city is there-- and add to the metropolitan burden of unemployment and underemployment.

The urban structure of most of the developing countries is highly condensed--in a few major centers (sometimes only one) linked by elemental railway and highway systems and surrounded by vast rural areas whose people subsist in premodern agricultural economies, often with feudal or semifeudal systems

of control. Urban culture and technology are
concentrated in the centers and, narrowly, along the
railways and major roads, fading out rapidly away
from these arteries of information.

This skeletal urbanism exists typically in a
regional context in which rural education, health
services, and communication are still largely
medieval--delaying the transformation of the rural
economy and failing to prepare the migrant for the
urban life to which he flees.

Administrative systems in the rural areas (and,
in some cases, even in urban areas) often belong to
a "predevelopment" era in the sense that they are
organized and operated as policing systems (following
the earlier colonial patterns) rather than development
systems. Shifts to a development focus and the
creation of development skills and attitudes are
only now emerging.

The political contexts of urbanization in the
developing countries vary greatly and are extremely
complex. In some cases, political power is still
concentrated in the elites, both rural and urban,
with a very narrow "public" base. In other cases,
the rural voter is by no means controlled by the old
elite. In all cases, the assemblies where major
formal political decisions are made are in the
metropolitan areas, and it generally is in the urban
centers that the ideas that bring political change
emerge. The leading activists go out on sorties
from the city to their constituencies.

What roles can the metropolis play in development, and how well is it prepared to play them?
Conditions vary greatly among the developing
countries, but the following reflections are true
of most of them:

a) The metropolis contains a major concentration
of the productive capacity through which the economic
condition of the nation can be improved relatively
rapidly, at least in the short run. The manufacturing
and trading heart of the nation is in its major
metropolitan areas. The existing industrial base of
the metropolis, its service base, the skilled labor
available there, and the markets provided by it make
it the major magnet for much new growth--for both
large-scale modern firms and embryo firms. São Paulo
contains approximately 45 per cent of the manufacturing

capacity of Brazil; in Panama 50 per cent of the total population of the country live within an hour's commuting distance of Panama City or Colon; in eastern India 42 per cent of the entire urban population of the four states of West Bengal, Bihar, Orissa, and Assam live within about an hour's commuting distance of the center of Calcutta. The pattern of concentration is being broken gradually by new industrial concentrations, as in the Damodar Valley and at Santo Tome de Guyana. The role of these new centers in long-run urbanization is very important; but in at least the immediate future, the existing major centers must continue to be major generators of change.

Many of the policies required to utilize the economic advantages of the metropolis to the full will have to be national and state policies, but metropolitan planning itself can substantially affect productivity in both the secondary and tertiary sectors.

On the debit side are urban unemployment and underemployment levels. A substantial part of the capital equipment of the major centers is obsolete, and extensive reorganization is needed in many sectors of their economies. There are serious bottlenecks and deficiencies in transportation, power, water, waste disposal, and a number of the other parts of the infrastructure required to optimize economic growth. Large amounts of potentially productive capital are tied up in urban land speculation.

b) Institutionally, the metropolis usually houses the central administrative functions of the nation or the region, and offers the most specialized services in such things as education and health. It houses the centralized elements of the nation's modern monetary institutions. It is a major communication center and a major generator of development-oriented attitudes and ideas. However, many of the services provided are premodern. Education and health are prominent among those services that are important for growth and almost universally inadequate. In the Calcutta Metropolitan District, for example, there are already 470,000 school children at the primary and junior secondary levels who should be attending school (according to the national target for education) but are not. In all the major metropolitan areas, premodern institutions exist alongside modern urban ones. Many major centers are, institutionally, collections of villages with a relatively modern institutional core. Many of the city's inhabitants do not have access to its modern institutions at all.

c)   The administrative functions of the
metropolis--national and regional as well as local--
make it vital as a center of administrative action.
It often is the origin of development ideas and
policies. Some of the most important development
(as opposed to policing) experience originates in the
metropolis because that is where renewal and growth
pressures are most severe; but urban administrative
structures and processes are generally inadequate.
Planning staffs are almost nonexistent. Implementing
authorities generally are not equipped to deal with
the scales of development problems they face. A
recent self-assessment of a major Latin American city
characterizes the administrative structure as being
thirty years out of date. For a number of other
centers, that would be an optimistic estimate.

d)   The metropolis is a center for both formal
and informal political activity. It typically is a
major origin of political ferment. It contains the
distillates of the nation's revolutionary ideas
juxtaposed with the most severe forms of the nation's
economic, social, and physical problems. Its physical
structures, in particular, provide compact and highly
visible opportunities for political symbolism--as in
Islamabad, Chandigarh, Brasilia, and Caracas.

e)   The provision of a physical base for urban
activity is, of course, one of the major functions of
the metropolis. It is also one that is being performed
lamentably in most of the developing countries. In one
major metropolitan area with a population of over
7.5 million, there is now less potable water per capita
than there was in the 1930's; only about 5 per cent of
the area is sewered. Almost all metropolitan transportation systems are already heavily congested, even
though automobile ownership is still in its infancy.
Housing, schools, and health facilities are desperately
inadequate. City building technology is a blend of the
ancient and modern. In many cases, construction is
slow and of poor quality. In almost all cases, the
maintenance of modern urban facilities is difficult
and precludes some of the building solutions that are
emerging in the relatively developed countries. On
the credit side, the low levels of physical city
building that have been achieved in a number of the
developing countries leave open very exciting
possibilities for long-run physical development--
possibilities that may be denied to the older
metropolises of Europe and North America. Central
area structural densities, though very high in some
locations, are interspersed with open space or

physical development of low intensity (though
population densities may nevertheless be high).
Much of the area surrounding the central core
typically is developed at a low physical intensity
and will be fairly readily renewable in the long run
if strategic areas are identified and controlled now.
Even medieval street systems that are abominably
congested now can be turned to good advantage later.

All of these factors suggest the importance of
focusing a large part of the immediate development
effort on existing major urban centers. Although it
is important to focus effort also on the creation of
new industrial and urban centers, their initiation
will at first have to draw heavily on existing major
centers for commodities, services, and skilled
personnel. Existing metropolitan areas are therefore
likely to have to play a key role in both urban and
regional development in the immediate future.

AN OUTLINE OF A STRATEGY FOR
METROPOLITAN PLANNING AND DEVELOPMENT

In such a context, what kinds of metropolitan
planning strategy seem promising? As a preliminary
to exploring this question, it is important to
establish the boundaries of the present discussion.
Metropolitan planning should be carried out in
conjunction with effective national and state (or
other subregional) planning. But the focus here is
on metropolitan planning itself. Regional planning
barely exists in an effective form in either the
advanced or the developing countries, but both it
and submetropolitan planning require separate
discussions beyond the scope of this one.

The present focus is also on the kinds of
planning that will be required in the immediate
future. A long-range view might call for different
emphases and allocate the planning effort among
metropolitan and other agencies in a different way.
The concern here is with the issues that are pressing
and the planning capacities that it is likely to be
possible to create, for political as well as
technical reasons, fairly quickly.

For the metropolis itself, a distinction can be
drawn between all governmental planning and development in the metropolis and planning and development
by the metropolitan government (or the major municipal

government or governments if, as is usually the case,
there is no metropolitan unit). A vital part of the
planning and development in the metropolis will, of
course, be private, but our concern is with
governmental activity.

Much of all the governmental planning in the
metropolitan area will be executed by state and
national governments and directed to state or
national objectives. Planning by the metropolitan
or other local governments will be directed to local
objectives but may also be supporting those of the
higher levels of government. It is usual to say that
national, state, and local planning should be
coordinated. This often presupposes the existence
or possibility of a single and internally consistent
set of development objectives supported by all levels
of government. In practice, the several levels of
government are likely to have conflicting objectives,
and the various local governments that constitute the
metropolis are themselves likely to be pursuing
different ends. Specific concerns may be different,
even if general party ideologies coincide. In some
cases, different party groups may dominate at
different levels.

Even with party uniformity, national and local
objectives may conflict (for example, in their
concerns with income distribution); and the long-
term interests of the nation may be at odds with those
of the metropolis, even if their short-run objectives
are consistent.

A limited amount of consistency sometimes is
achieved by indirection or default. Some national
or state concerns are reflected in local planning
because local political leaders aspire to state or
national office. In a number of cases, local
governments are so weak that the state takes direct
responsibility for metropolitan planning, and state
concerns receive attention at the local level
because of this. In a few cases, there are
intergovernmental policy groups explicitly
responsible for coordinating activities at the
metropolitan level, but this is the exception
rather than the rule.

Our attention here is directed to situations
in which there exists, or is to be created, an
agency expressly responsible for over-all metropolitan
planning. The question of whether national and state

interests are pursued directly by this agency, or
recognized as factors affecting metropolitan development in conjunction with the local objectives pursued
by the metropolitan agency, will be left open.
Although the specific range of objectives for which
the metropolitan agency is responsible will affect
the work load and detailed composition of the agency's
staff, this does not affect the points that are to be
made.   (Moreover, the differences in work load will
be smaller now than later on because national and
state objectives in the developing countries generally
are not translated into localized metropolitan
components clearly enough to relieve the local agency
of the burden of identifying their metropolitan
implications.)

The strategy that is to be suggested will be
discussed in four parts: the objectives of
metropolitan planning; the scope of the planning
required; the establishment of a framework for
metropolitan planning and development; and the
roles of policy-makers, publics, administrators,
and planners.

The Objectives of Metropolitan Planning

The following list of objectives that may be
pursued through metropolitan development is by no
means exhaustive, but it will suffice as a context
for the subsequent part of the discussion.

Income Growth

For the reasons suggested earlier, it is likely
that an important part of immediately necessary
increases in secondary and tertiary output and income
can be achieved most effectively through additions to
capacity in major metropolitan areas. Many of the
decisions determining additions to capacity will
originate, of course, at the national or state,
rather than the local, level. However, increases in
capacity and productivity also can be induced by
improvements in metropolitan services and facilities--
such as transportation, water supply and waste
disposal, technical and general education, health,
and housing--that expand capacity directly or alter
the production functions of firms in the metropolitan
area. (For specific industries and specific localities, the question of whether incremental additions
to urban infrastructure are most productive in major
metropolitan areas or elsewhere is, however, still
largely open.)

In the past, many firms, particularly foreign ones, have provided much of their own infrastructure, for reasons of security as well as efficiency. The public provision of better infrastructure shifts the cost burden. Even if it is not more efficient for the infrastructure itself, it may induce the creation of new capacity that would not otherwise have developed at all. Coupled with improvements in governmental provisions for security and adequate political stability, it can be of particular importance in encouraging foreign investment.

Increases in investment in productive capacity in metropolitan areas can also be induced through appropriate changes in tax policies--not only by adjusting corporate and individual income taxes directly, but also, in many cases, through changes in land tax policies (for example, by shifting from a tax on present income on urban property to a tax on the market value of the property).

Increases in manufacturing capacity, service capacity, and the supply of skilled manpower in the metropolis are important for their impact on metropolitan income and output; they are important also because they generate some of the inputs required for increasing output in lesser urban centers and in agriculture.

Employment

Increases in metropolitan output beyond those that arise through increases in productivity will usually be associated with increased employment. However, the major metropolitan areas in the developing countries are likely to be major centers of unemployment and underemployment for a substantial part of the foreseeable future. Their dominance attracts rural to urban migrants whether there are definite job offers or not. One can only hope that there is a reasonably rapid turnover in the unemployed group, so that its membership at any one time consists chiefly of recent migrants or the recently unemployed. The metropolis can be an effective generator of employment, even though it has a permanent unemployment pool. (It can, similarly, be an effective generator of increased incomes, at least in the short run, even though an influx of low-income migrants may lower statistically the per capita income of the metropolitan population.)

Improved Consumption Patterns

Increases in the consumption of critical goods and services, such as food, shelter, education, and health care, can be effected in the metropolis not only through higher incomes and increases in the production of these goods and services, but also through decreases in their real costs and/or the real costs of other commodities. Some community-wide decreases in real costs can be achieved through improvements in metropolitan organization. For groups in the population whose needs are especially great, consumption patterns can be improved by reducing costs for these groups specifically--not only by the familiar types of subsidy, but also by making the goods and services more accessible. Their physical accessibility can be improved by improving the physical organization of the city; their psychological, social, and political accessibility can be improved by creating institutions that will make them more accessible.

Increases in Human Potential

The rather awkward term "human potential" is used, for want of a better one, for all of the human characteristics that affect an individual's capacity for productive activity and pleasure in the future. These include such things as his knowledge, his health, and his skills.

The provision of vocational and general education health services, and a variety of urban institutional services is important in the creation of such potentia. Particularly important in the developing areas are the institutions that help to acculturate the migrant to urban life. Just as important are the institutions that make the metropolis a major source of the most specialized kinds of information. Because the metropolis is a breeding ground for modernization, the ideas and skills originating in it are important not only for the city dweller but for the nation as a whole.

Improved Administration

Improvements in administration can be regarded as instrumentally valuable, rather than important in themselves. They are mentioned specifically here because of their critical importance in the development of the metropolis itself and because the

metropolis can serve very effectively as a training
ground for administrators who will later work in
other urban areas.

Political Objectives

The devices through which the nature and distribution of political power and conflict can be affected
in metropolitan development are numerous, and only a
few that have to do directly with metropolitan
planning will be mentioned here. One is the pattern
of political sub-units in which the community is
organized, for this will affect the degrees to which
particular parts of the population have access to
the political power structure. Another is the
physical form of the metropolis. This, as noted
earlier, can serve as a major source of political
symbolism. A recent study suggests also that the
physical layout of the city can affect significantly
the probability of conflict.[1] A third is the range
of choices of activity and residence provided in
the metropolis. A fourth is the set of institutions
provided for the resolution of conflict. A fifth is
the set of regulations that govern the use and
transfer of property.

Aesthetic Objectives

It might be argued that no developing country
can afford to worry about aesthetic objectives while
it is struggling desperately to avoid economic and
social disaster. It is true that too much attention
has been given to the physiognomy of the city in
urban planning doctrine (though not in practice) in
the past. The physical form of the metropolis has
been a major source of human delight or despair in
the past and will continue to be in the future. To
reproduce carelessly the ugliness that typifies
metropolitan areas in the developed countries--
presumably to pass later through similarly agonized
attempts at rejuvenation--would be inexcusable.
Low intensities of physical development in a number
of metropolitan areas in the developing countries
leave open opportunities to create urban forms more
exciting than any that have occurred in the past.
There is no reason to believe that these cannot be
approached gradually through a series of forms
appropriate at each stage to the local cultural and
economic condition. Reassuringly, evidence that this
is possible lies in some of the developing countries
themselves, as well as in transferable building methods
that are emerging from relatively developed industrial
economies.

The Scope of the Planning Required

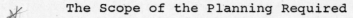

Metropolitan planning that is to be directed toward objectives of these kinds is clearly very complex and much broader in scope than the city planning that has been attempted to date in North America or Europe. It cannot be the responsibility of a single type of urban planner. Clearly, it calls for a great variety of planning and development skills.

In the immediate future, the metropolitan agency is likely to have to do a large part of the regional planning that is required as a context for metropolitan decisions--in part because no one else is doing it and in part because initial buildups of urban planning skill are likely to occur in the metropolitan areas. For metropolitan planning itself, it will be necessary to identify and extract skillfully from national and state programs not only the policies that have a direct bearing on metropolitan development but also a wide variety of data and analyses that can be used locally. Such planning, therefore, calls for a sound understanding of national economic planning and a capacity for regional planning at least sufficient to establish a context for metropolitan planning.

It calls for a sound understanding of the locational behavior of firms in each of the industry groups that is relevant for the metropolis--and the special factors affecting the locational decisions of foreign firms.

There must be an understanding of consumer behavior and the ways in which consumption patterns can be expected to change in response to public investment in facilities and services.

There must be a capacity for the development of sound fiscal policy. The metropolitan consequences of state and national tax policies must be anticipated. Metropolitan fiscal policies must be designed to encourage the kinds of land development that are sought.

The technologies of services, such as education and health, must be understood as a basis for recommending effective programs in these fields, as must institutional opportunities for accelerating the processes through which rural to urban migrants can adapt successfully to urban life.

Most aspects of metropolitan administration need
intensive modernization and expansion. This will be
especially true of development agencies. Though they
are engaged in piecemeal implementation now, many of
them are drastically inadequate for the scales of
renewal and new construction that have to be faced.
Major planning efforts will be pointless if appropriate
implementing agencies are not developed simultaneously.

If political stability is of prime concern, then
economic planning for the metropolis, the planning of
social services, land use legislation, and the
planning of the physical environment must be designed
to encourage stability. The timing of development
may have to be programed to highlight or subdue
critical political issues.

The transportation needs of the metropolis must
be anticipated, as must the impact of transportation
on land use and opportunities for substituting
communication for transportation.

These are only a few of the things that must
fall within the purview of those engaged in effective
metropolitan planning. The listing here has been
purposely biased by including hardly any of the
traditional concerns of city planning, though they
are all important, to emphasize a point. Effective
metropolitan planning must be much more than
broadminded municipal engineering. It deals with an
elaborate system whose economy, social institutions,
governmental structure, and physical environment must
be acted upon to focus the drive for development.
The kinds of intervention required are largely those
for which urban planning training and practice hardly
prepare the professional planner at all. The tradition
in city planning in Europe and North America has been
to regard the physical environment as the main area
of professional concern--the economic, social, and
political systems of the city being somehow outside
the scope of planning. Meanwhile, of course, the
metropolis has been planned and changed continually
by private interest groups, by departments of finance,
by boards of education, health departments, highway
departments, and the like. In the developing
countries, the programs of many public agencies have
been very limited. In both the developing countries
and the relatively developed ones, they have been
largely unconnected.

The Establishment of a Framework
for Metropolitan Planning and Development

It is said that once a problem is well
described, considerable progress has been made
toward its solution. For effective metropolitan
planning and development, what is desirable is a
thorough description of all the decisions that have
to be made in preparing and implementing a continuing
program, the ways in which those decisions should be
logically connected with one another, and the events
that are expected to result from them. Such a
description should be based on a thorough understanding of the way in which the metropolitan system
functions and the points at which it can be entered
most effectively to guide its growth in accord with
public policy. The analytical tools required for
this should be designed to serve the following
purposes, among others:

a) to facilitate the structuring of all of
the major economic, social, legislative, administrative, and environmental factors that need to be
considered in developing policies for metropolitan
systems; the tools should help to structure them in
such a way as to identify the linkages that should
be recognized in formulating policies and in such a
way as to differentiate clearly policy objectives,
policy instruments, and constraints.

b) to help in identifying the clusters in
which economic, social, environmental, and other
factors should be analyzed for policy purposes. The
factors clustered together should be clustered
because of the logical interdependence of the
decisions that have to be made about them. If
distinct clusters are identifiable, it should
reflect the fact that decisions about each cluster
can be made sequentially in the policy-making process
(that is, they do not have to be decided simultaneously). The identification of such clusters can
be of help not only in breaking a very complex
problem down into more manageable subproblems but
also in assigning specific clusters of decision-
making responsibilities to specific agencies.

c) to assist in identifying efficient sequences
for analyzing such clusters in formulating and
evaluating policies.

d)   to assist in identifying strategic entry points in complex metropolitan systems and/or the larger systems of which they are parts--entry points at which governmental and private policies of particular kinds are likely to be most effective.

e)   to assist in identifying the paths along which the impacts of particular types of policies are likely to be transmitted in urban systems.

f)   to assist in evaluating alternative policies by identifying their likely consequences, both qualitative and quantitative.

g)   to assist in defining the boundaries of metropolitan and other regions that can be used as effective policy units.

h)   to assist in assessing the vulnerability of specific communities to economic and social disruption that may arise from governmental or private action.

i)   to assist in assessing the adaptability of specific communities to changes in policy that are being considered by various levels of government; the tools proposed should help to identify not only the types of change that are likely to be generated by particular policies but also the capacity of a community to retain its identity under such changes.

Such a description would be invaluable in identifying the kinds of skill required for planning and development and the ways in which they should be organized. It would be invaluable for tracing the likely consequences of decisions made about any particular element in the metropolitan system. It would assist in selecting the elements to be worked with in executing public policies for long-range development. It would be useful also as a day-to-day urban management tool (for example, in tracing quickly the likely consequences of pending policy changes; in tracing the likely paths of social disturbances initiated at particular points in the system, assessing the likelihood of massive buildups of activity, and the places at which ameliorative action is likely to be most effective).

Such a description of the problem is, of course, much easier to recommend than it is to achieve. There is not yet a good vocabulary for denoting the individual elements of metropolitan systems, let alone the understanding required to describe the relationships among those elements.

The kind of analysis that might be utilized has been developed in a preliminary form by the author. It has been applied, for illustrative purposes, to a very small segment (of only forty-two elements) of the Calcutta Metropolitan District planning problem, in which the author was engaged between 1964-67.[2]

This type of procedure will yield more sensitive results as our understanding of metropolitan structures and processes improves, but it can be used immediately with present levels of understanding and data in the developing countries. The inter-relationships among the elements of metropolitan systems are very complex even when described with the crude knowledge and data available now. They are very difficult to analyze systematically. Without a device of this kind, the risks of overlooking important connections are great. It is difficult to organize efficiently for planning; it is also difficult to respond to impending crises quickly at the most effective points in the metropolitan structure.

A work program for the management of both the planning and development operations is another essential part of the equipment needed for effective guidance of metropolitan growth. It should identify, in sequence, all of the decisions and actions that have to be performed from the stage of initial problem identification through the identification of operational objectives, program formulation, implementation, and evaluation. It should identify all of the significant actions to be performed, not only in the planning and implementing agencies but also in maintaining effective public relations, in the development of legislation, in the legislative processing of proposals, and in all of the functions that have to be performed in the course of planning and development. The work program should identify also the participants, both public and private, who should be involved in each part of the over-all process and the data inputs required at each stage. An analytical procedure of the kind described will form an important part of the basis for work programing.

In conjunction with analytical frameworks and
work programs of the kinds just described, governments
concerned with urban and regional planning should
establish urban information systems designed to
provide both the public and private groups involved
in planning and development with the up-to-date
information they need for each phase of their
activities.

Metropolitan systems are becoming increasingly
complex, and there is a great variety of economic,
social, administrative, and environmental data that
must be organized systematically and made available
readily on an up-to-date basis if metropolitan growth
is to be guided effectively. The traditional methods
of processing planning and development information
are no longer adequate. Governmental information
systems are overloaded. It may take months to get
information that could be available in a matter of
minutes. In many cases, valuable information is
lost altogether because of poor methods of collection,
processing, and storage.

In the developing areas, in particular, the
problem is not only one of overload. Many of the
most basic types of data required for effective
metropolitan planning do not exist at all or do not
exist in an up-to-date form.

There is a critical need for a well-designed
urban data system or collection of systems to serve
metropolitan planning and implementation. Such
systems should be linked with their counterparts at
the national, state, and local levels. They should
be designed to provide for the effective collection,
processing, storage, and retrieval of critical
information. They should circulate information
regularly on an up-to-date basis to a variety of
users. What is needed is not only "a better set of
data" but a better set of processes for maintaining
regular flows of critical data. The quality of
metropolitan planning in the developing areas could
be improved dramatically, even without more
sophisticated analytical tools, simply by having a
better informational environment to provide a
basis for sound decisions.

The development of such systems should be
gradual and addressed always to the most critical
policy-making needs. The pattern and pace of
development must be sensitive to local capacities

for adapting new techniques. Systems should be kept
as simple and efficient as possible in all stages of
development. In most cases, they should begin with
a better utilization of existing facilities and
procedures rather than an immediate move to computerization on a large scale. It is important to avoid the
pitfalls of the elaborate "data banks" that have been
created in the United States and elsewhere--massive
collections of material that were assembled more
because of the existence of sophisticated computer
equipment than because of a concern with specific
policy issues. In a number of cases, urban areas in
the United States are only now trying to decide what
to do with the complex data they have collected.
They have arrived at "answers" without having framed
questions.

It would be embarrassing to describe the simple-
minded basis for action that has just been discussed
without developing it more fully if it were not for
the fact that the three planning tools identified--a
problem description structured in a particular way,
a comprehensive work program, and an information
system for planning and development--have nowhere
(in the developed countries or the developing ones)
been created and used coherently, even with the data
and knowledge presently available.

On the basis of the context and metropolitan
planning objectives established earlier, the
prescription for a planning strategy can be carried
one step further. Metropolitan areas in the
developing countries are growing rapidly in the face
of urgent economic, social, and physical problems of
awesome dimensions. In most cases, there is no long-
range perspective identifying directions for
metropolitan growth; but government agencies at
various levels are, nevertheless, implementing
fragmentary schemes as quickly as possible under the
pressures of impending crises. In almost all cases,
the machinery for adequate metropolitan planning and
development barely exists.

Given this situation, it seems reasonable to
suggest that the planning and development effort
should consist of at least three parts, to be
initiated immediately and developed simultaneously:
immediate action programing; long-range programing;
and the development of planning and implementing
machinery.

Immediate Action Programing

The programing and implementation executed under
this heading should be concerned with solutions for
the metropolitan area's most pressing problems. Some
of the programs developed will have to be implemented
before there is any long-range program. Initially
they will have to be based on the considered judgments
of people both inside and outside government who
already know the metropolis well, plus whatever data
are already available. There will be little or no
time for new surveys. Programs will have to be
translated quickly from general ideas into detailed
and implementable recommendations. Later, detailed
short-range programing based on the current long-
range program and relatively thorough information
will become a normal feature of the planning process,
intermediary between long-range general planning and
implementation. The professional staff involved in
immediate action programing should be relatively
senior and experienced, capable of making sound
judgments quickly, and capable of establishing
effective liaisons quickly with the governmental
and private groups that should be involved.

Programing of this kind will be essential for
responding to urgent economic, social, physical, and
political concerns. It will be important also where
the planning function is new for establishing public
and governmental confidence in the planning agency.
The results of the immediate action programs will
provide important evaluative material for improving
long-range programing. They will be valuable also
in designing the machinery for sustained planning
and implementation.

Long-Range Programing

Long-range programing should establish on a
continuing basis the directions the growth of the
metropolis should take over a period of fifteen to
twenty years, the actual time horizon depending on
the nature of the individual area and the data that
are available. Within the over-all period, there
should be a series of intermediate time horizons,
corresponding with national and state planning
periods (for the purposes of analysis as well as
budgeting), with a financing program for at least
the first intermediate period of about five years.
As the time period becomes more remote, the range of
alternatives implicit in each intermediate program

is likely to increase because of the increasing
uncertainty associated with more remote periods.
The identification of intermediate programs is
important for the planning agency itself in assessing
the realism of long-range targets; it is important in
demonstrating the realism of the over-all program when
support for it is being sought; and it will be an
important aid in switching from one development path
to another if conditions or objectives change.

Long-range programing with a broad national and
regional perspective is essential because of the
interdependence of national, regional, and metropolitan
development. It is essential also because of the need
to plan soundly those incremental investments which
commit the government to major long-run investments
and/or operating and maintenance expenditures. As
an aspect of this, it is necessary to demonstrate
(one hopes) the rationality of the judgments made in
immediate action programing--in some cases, the
rationality of changing the directions implied by
earlier decisions for immediate action, even though
these may still appear to be reasonable when viewed
in a short-range perspective. It is essential for
discounting the expected costs and returns of long-
life projects in a way that will reflect properly
their interdependencies. One of its major virtues
may, of course, be that it yields insights into
possibilities for forms of economic, social,
political, and physical change quite different from
the past or the short-range future--thus guiding
immediate investment in directions which do not
build into the metropolitan system rigidities based
chiefly on the past.

In most cases, it will be essential to develop
a first long-range program very quickly; and this,
like the immediate action programs, will have to be
based chiefly on sound local judgment and data
already available, rather than on major new research.
The commitments made in early versions of the long-
range program will, therefore, have to strike a nice
compromise between providing a sufficient basis for
immediate action and remaining open to the possibilities that may emerge as the machinery for planning
is improved.

The Development of Planning and Implementing Machinery

The overriding importance of establishing
adequate implementing machinery as a prerequisite

for productive planning has been stressed already.
In addition to establishing an administrative system
that is appropriate in scale and organization for the
immense metropolitan development task, a major effort
will have to be made in most cases to train administrative personnel in modern methods of management for
their various specialized functions. It is essential
also that they be exposed to the issues and possibilities of over-all urbanization and the functions of the
metropolitan planning agency in a way that will make
it possible for them to integrate their own planning
with the work of the metropolitan agency.

The planning machinery itself is likely to be
almost nonexistent at first. It obviously is
important to develop a sufficient staff for the most
urgent tasks, and this is likely to be done reasonably
quickly. However, even in the immediate future, the
burden of intergovernmental, interdepartmental, and
interdisciplinary mobilization is likely to be
considerable, and additional training for the
planning staff probably will be required.

What is not likely to be so readily recognized
or budgeted for is the essential research, training,
and institutionalizing activity that should be
initiated immediately to prepare the way for
consistent improvements in the quality of planning
and the effective integration of the planning function
in the established structure of government. It is
perfectly reasonable to develop the first immediate
action programs and long-range programs on a very
slender basis, but planning and development cannot
proceed effectively if each successive stage of
programing is based on little more knowledge than
the preceding one. The costs of operating from a
poor information base, coupled with weak analytic
tools, are likely to increase as the metropolis grows.
As the obverse of this, the marginal returns from
improvements in information and techniques are likely
to be much greater in the developing countries than
they are in the relatively developed ones.

The maturation of effective research techniques
and planning procedures for the developing countries
will take considerable time. Some of the tools and
techniques developed elsewhere will be directly
transferable, others will have to be modified
considerably, and many new ones will have to be
created. An explicit staff and budget for research
should be provided as an integral part of the
initiation of improved planning. A variety of kinds

of training in and outside the planning agency will
be required, and this also should be budgeted for
explicitly with a separate training staff and/or
explicit time set aside for training by qualified
members of the operating staff. It cannot be
assumed that adequate training will somehow "rub off"
in the everday work of the agency. The particular
approaches to training that are likely to be most
effective are covered in Chapter 5.

The Roles of Policy-Makers, Publics, Administrators, and Planners

The roles of each of these four types of
participants in development will differ from place
to place, partly with differences in governmental
structure and, for the public (or publics) in
particular, with the local culture and the stage of
economic development.

For the reasons suggested earlier, the levels
of government that are critical in the metropolis
may be different in different instances. Often in
the immediate future, the state or national government
will be dominant, though in a few cases local governments are strong enough to control their own planning
and development functions effectively already.

In most cases, there will be no effective general
public exerting pressure for metropolitan improvement
and no general public to which the government can
appeal for support in conducting metropolitan affairs.
Instead, there are likely to be fragmented collections
of special-interest publics, some highly organized
and powerful, many in loose alliances. This is true
for metropolitan areas in the relatively developed
countries also, but the degree of fragmentation in
the developing countries is much greater, and the
potential for the creation of a general public with
a sustained interest in metropolitan affairs much less.
Therefore, initial mobilization for planning and
development often must be achieved through the elites
and the relatively few public groups that already are
well organized and powerful, though an attempt should
be made to lay the groundwork for more widespread
participation where this is consistent with the
nation's political values.

Both the metropolitan planning agency and a wide
range of administrative agencies must, of course, play
major roles in planning and development, but there is

relatively little need for the North American kind
of generalist planner. Several points need to be
emphasized:

a) The training and experience of the typical
North American generalist by no means equip him for
guiding metropolitan planning of the kind discussed
here. He does not know enough about any of the
specialized urban functions to plan for them or
coordinate their planning well. Nor does he know
enough about management and complex systems planning
techniques to be able to coordinate effectively the
diverse planning activities that together could
constitute effective governmental action. There is
a need for a particular kind of generalist, one who
is skilled in management and over-all systems
planning, but he is not the kind of generalist urban
planner that has emerged in North America to date.

b) Even if the right kinds of generalists can
be found or trained, relatively few of them will be
needed in the developed or the developing countries,
though the few that are needed will have to be
exceptionally good.

c) The bulk of the metropolitan planning task
is likely to be executed most effectively by
specialist planners working in their own fields--
either in the metropolitan planning agency or in a
diversity of administrative agencies. The
perspectives of at least the key people in these
specialist planning groups must be broad enough for
them to recognize the ways in which their own
activities are related to the major issues and
opportunities of urbanization. The key specialists
must also be competent in planning and/or management
in their own fields and able to collaborate effectively
in the over-all planning effort led by the metropolitan agency.

d) In quantitative terms, by far the greater
part of the effort required to improve the quality
of metropolitan planning and development should be
directed at the administrative agencies in the
immediate future, rather than planning agencies
per se. The development of a special cadre of
competent urban administrators and administrative
agency staffs should be supported as actively as
possible, though this will, in some cases, require
a departure from ascendance in the traditional
generalist administrative hierarchy and the

ascription of much higher status to the urban
specialist. Several of these points are developed
more fully in Chapter 3.

The face of urban America, and much more than
the face, has been changed by the specialists. In
reaction to the disasters they have contrived in their
worst, and regrettably repetitive, moments, we have
sought a cure in comprehensive and general planning--
but the generalists have been relatively ineffective.
In addition to the misdirected emphasis that has been
placed on the physical environment, the mistake has
been twofold: we have failed to broaden the
perspective of the specialist, and we have produced
the wrong kind of generalist. It is a mistake the
developing countries need not, and can scarcely
afford to, repeat.

NOTES TO CHAPTER 2

1. Richard L. Meier, "Policies for Urban
Settlements Intended to Minimize Losses from
Conflict and Violence" (paper presented at a
seminar in cooperation with the United States
Public Health Service, The Role of Science in
Environmental Planning, May 25-27, 1966).

2. For a full description of the method
proposed, see the Ph.D. dissertation, University
of Pennsylvania, 1964, of John D. Herbert,
A Procedure for the Articulation of Complex
Development Programming Problems, Ann Arbor, Michigan:
University Microfilms, 1965), espec. pp. 142-66.

CHAPTER **3** URBAN DEVELOPMENT
ADMINISTRATION:
THE CASE OF JAPAN

Masahiko Honjo*

INTRODUCTION

Because of Japan's success in achieving rapid
economic development, there has been considerable
interest in her planning methods and in the various
legislative and administrative measures that have
been developed there. Our review of her development
will include analyses of the important contributions
made by national comprehensive development planning,
city planning, and housing planning.

NATIONAL COMPREHENSIVE DEVELOPMENT PLANNING

In a consideration of Japanese urban planning,
it is important to recognize how administrative
responsibility is divided between the central and
the local governments. Japan was modernized rapidly
after the Meiji Restoration, and the government
played a leading role in strengthening industrial
activities and military power through centralized
administration. Local government administration was
based on the prefecture, which was a revised form of
the feudal clan system. The prefectures were
controlled by governors appointed by the central
government, and they, in turn, controlled the
municipalities.

---

*Masahiko Honjo, B.A., is a Member of the Board
of Directors of PADCO, Inc., and a Professor in the
Department of Urban Engineering, Tokyo University.

After World War II, the administrative system was revised again. The local citizens began electing the governors, and local administration became more democratic. At the same time, however, the necessity for postwar reconstruction imposed a large financial demand on the locality. Changes in the taxation system have not yet met this demand. Hence, the local governments are, to a large extent, dependent on the central government for financial resources, with the result that local administrations still tend to be influenced heavily by the central government in their decision-making.

In addition, the postwar increase in urban populations accelerated the growth of metropolitan regions, forming conurbations that extended beyond existing administrative boundaries. The concurrent increase in economic activities resulted in a closer interconnection of local prefectures. Today, Japan faces the problem of reorganizing existing administrative boundaries and redividing decision-making responsibilities among the several levels of government.

Part of the difficulty in arriving at a satisfactory reallocation of powers arises from the unevenness of the distribution of local resources and capacities. Secondary and tertiary industries progressed rapidly in the Pacific corridor that connects Tokyo, Nagoya, and Osaka, hence centering population in these areas. Industrialization, growth in income, and urbanization proceeded hand in hand. A comparison of the income per capita by prefectures and the proportion of population engaged in secondary and tertiary industries will show this trend clearly (Graph 1).

Gaps between developed and underdeveloped prefectures, naturally, are reflected in the prefectures' available finances. In the postwar taxation system, the main sources of income for the local authorities are the property tax, the inhabitant tax, and the sales tax. However, the total receipts do not equal expenditures. Additional sums are acquired from the central government, which distributes a part of the national tax income as an equalization grant to prefectures, according to their economic potential and financial needs. Subsidies for major public works also are distributed to local authorities through the ministries concerned.

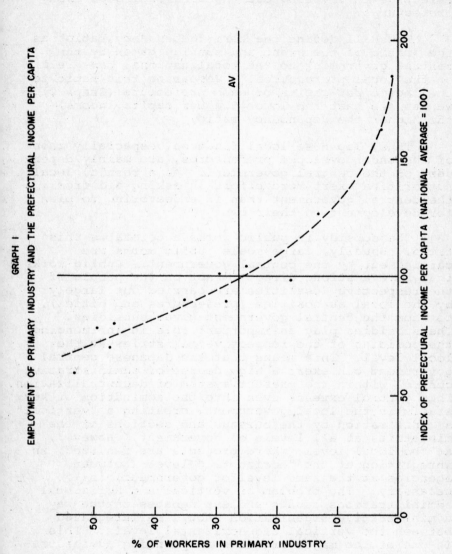

GRAPH I

EMPLOYMENT OF PRIMARY INDUSTRY AND THE PREFECTURAL INCOME PER CAPITA

% OF WORKERS IN PRIMARY INDUSTRY

INDEX OF PREFECTURAL INCOME PER CAPITA (NATIONAL AVERAGE = 100)

AV

Source: Saburo Okita et al., Regional Society and Urban Agglomeration.
(Tokyo: Kajima Press, 1967), p. 188

These grants and subsidies are, to some extent, effective in leveling out the financial gaps among prefectures.

We shall define the term "dependency ratio" as the "ratio of the grant and subsidy given by the central government to the total national tax yield of the local prefectures." Comparing this ratio to the income per capita of each prefecture (Graph 2), we can see that the lower the per capita income, the higher the dependency ratio.

Thus, Japanese local finances, especially those of the underdeveloped prefectures, are mainly dependent on the central government. As a result, local authorities exert more effort in asking aid from the central government than in endeavoring to plan for development on their own.

The subsidy in public works accelerates this trend. Usually, large-scale public works are carried out by the central government. Public works that have a strong direct impact on the people of the respective localities are carried out largely by the local authorities (prefectures and cities), to whom the central government gives subsidies. The subsidies play an important role in influencing the policies of the respective ministries at the local level. This means that the Japanese central government can exert a high degree of administrative control within the present system of decentralization. This control extends even into the nomination of key staffs in the local government, creating a "vertical" administration by the bureaus and sections of the ministries at all levels of government. However, at the local level, where projects are realized, an integration at the "horizontal" level (between agencies at the same level of government) is necessary. The problem of vertical and horizontal administrations causes endless debates on the way administrative organization should be integrated between the vertical and horizontal levels. This is one of the major problems in planning administration. The recent trend is for the development of horizontal integration agencies or "units" at each level of the government: central, regional, and prefectural. At present, these agencies are not yet operating particularly well, but their role in a new phase of administration deserves further discussion.

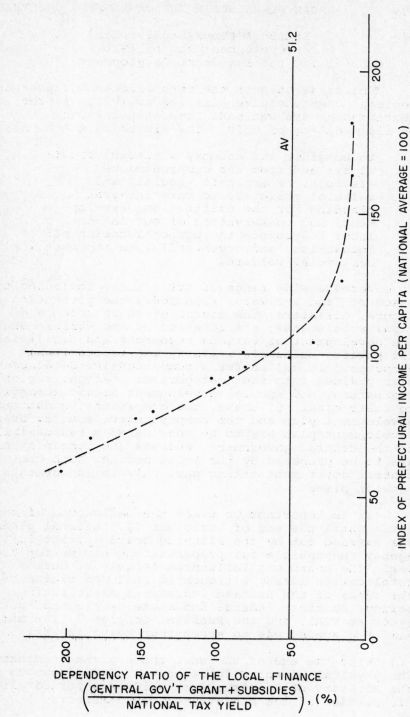

GRAPH 2

THE DEPENDENCY RATIO OF THE LOCAL FINANCE AND THE PREFECTURAL INCOME PER CAPITA

DEPENDENCY RATIO OF THE LOCAL FINANCE
$\left(\dfrac{\text{CENTRAL GOV'T GRANT + SUBSIDIES}}{\text{NATIONAL TAX YIELD}}\right)$, (%)

INDEX OF PREFECTURAL INCOME PER CAPITA (NATIONAL AVERAGE = 100)

Source: Saburo Okita et al., Regional Society and Urban Agglomeration.
(Tokyo: Kajima Press, 1967), p. 208.

39

National Comprehensive Land
Development Act of 1950
and the Resultant Development

The first step in the consolidation of postwar
regional comprehensive planning activity was the
enactment of the National Comprehensive Land
Development Act of 1950. The aim of this Act was

> to consider our country's natural condi-
> tions; and from the comprehensive
> viewpoint of economic, social, and
> cultural policies, to make integral
> planning for the utilization, develop-
> ment, and conservation of our national
> land; to promote the proper location of
> industries; and, eventually, to improve
> our social welfare.

It covered a wide range of activities, including the
usage of land and water resources; the prevention of
natural disasters; the distribution of urban and
rural settlements; the location of industries; and
the development of various resources and facilities
for public, cultural, welfare, and recreational
purposes. It called for a comprehensive development
plan divided into four categories: nation, region,
prefecture, and special development areas, according
to their size. Of these, the comprehensive national
development plan and the comprehensive special areas
development plan are to be considered a responsibility
of the central government, whereas the remaining plans
are to be prepared by the local bodies, with the
central government taking part only in adjustments
between plans.

It is important to trace the background of this
Act. Until the end of World War II, national planning
was carried out by the Planning Board (Kikaku-in), an
agency responsible for preparing the nation for "total
war. The Board was influenced largely by German
totalitarian ideas, although it included traits of
the ideas of the British industrial distribution
policy, American federal and state development policy
(such as TVA), and the Russian "Gosplan." The main
aim of planning was to strengthen heavy industry.

With the end of the war, these plans terminated.
The physical planning function was handed down to
the Ministry of Construction, which was formed after
dissolution of the Ministry of House Affairs.

Here, planning studies concentrated on reconstruction
works, emphasizing the development of natural
resources in the underdeveloped areas. The people
of these areas, who felt that they had been left
behind when the development of public works was under
the control of the central government, hoped that
resources development planning--even with its
emphasis on agriculture, forestry, and water
resources--would pull them out of backwardness.
It was this consensus at the local level that grew
into the political power that promoted the enactment
of the 1950 Act.

During the same period, the central government,
pressed by the necessity to stabilize and reconstruct
the economy, organized a compact and strong planning
group called the Economic Stabilization Board. The
Board developed the first national plan, the Economy
Rehabilitation Plan, in 1948. This Plan was made
from a "central" point of view and included population estimates, industries and agriculture, and the
planning of social overhead investment. Its
principal aim was to reconstruct the economy through
the recovery of key industries, and its main emphasis
was placed on economic efficiency through maximum
use of the existing industrial centers.

The 1948 Economic Rehabilitation Plan broke
down the targets for development and investment by
respective regions. This was the point at which
the economic planning of the central government
started to establish links with the development
planning of the localities. The National Comprehensive Land Development Act of 1950 was passed as an
outgrowth of these two movements.

The primary political pressure that promoted
the enactment of this Act was a demand for minimizing
the differences between the developed and underdeveloped areas. The Act's designation of "special
development areas" was the vehicle for this.
Immediately after the passing of the Act, action
was taken to appoint thirteen special development
areas, and nine more have since been added. The
first special development areas were selected largely
because they were clearly underdeveloped in relation
to the rest of the country.

The national, regional, prefectural, and special
development area planning programs required in the
1950 Act were slow in developing. The original

ten-year target was not accomplished. This may have
been due partly to the rapid rate of economic growth,
but it probably was due largely to the fact that
Japanese planning simply was not yet mature enough
for the tasks that confronted it.

The National Comprehensive Land Development Act
of 1950 led to various regional plans. Preceding
the National Comprehensive Land Development Act of
1950, the Hokkaido Development Act was enacted to
expedite comprehensive development in Hokkaido, the
frontier island of the extreme north. Following this,
other regional development acts were passed, aimed
mainly at underdeveloped regions, such as Tohoku,
Shikoku, Kyushu, Chugoku, and Hokuriku. They stressed
the importance of developing the regions through
industrialization. They also stipulated that development planning be directly authorized by the cabinet--
an attempt to secure larger public works budgets with
special assistance from the central government.

In addition, acts were passed to assist the
development of specific regions with especially low
productivity, those subject to major natural
disasters and/or those whose development was
markedly lagging. The development acts for heavy
snow regions, for torrential-poor-soil regions, and
for isolated islands are examples. These acts all
aim at eradicating the lag of development in those
areas through the increased allocation of finance
to public works, together with an increase in the
rate of subsidy.

The areas covered by special acts eventually
covered a large part of the country. However, ten
years after passage of the National Comprehensive
Land Development Act of 1950 found no expected
increase in investment. During those years, the
main trend of the economy supported "high-growth"
type industries, with the result that, contrary to
the expectations of the residents of the underdeveloped areas, the gap between the regions widened.
Despite this, the objective of eradicating the
development gaps persists and is one of the basic
objectives in national comprehensive development
planning.

The 1960's "High-Growth" Period
and the Income-Doubling Plan

Late in the 1950's, the economy reached the rapid-growth stage, based on industries and promoted by large-scale investment in the private sector. Since the industries were largely dependent on import and export, they developed near the ports. At the same time, the energy base changed from coal to oil. Thus, the growing economy speeded up the development of the Pacific Coast Industrial Belt, which extends from Tokyo to the Inland Seacoast through Osaka and Nagoya.

In 1960, the government submitted the so-called Income-Doubling Plan as the revised economic base for the next ten years. This Plan favored further development of the advanced regions, especially the Pacific Coast Industrial Belt. Its basic provisions aimed at keeping the economy growing under the free capitalistic system.

This policy drew criticism from those who were advocates of the "gap-elimination" view. In response to their objections, the Underdevelopment Area Industrial Development Promotion Act (1961) and the New Industrial City Construction Promotion Act (1962) were enacted. They were aimed at nominating a limited number of areas and cities to be developed, with special assistance from the central government-- assistance through devices such as the intensification of public investment, the extension of public loans, and reductions in taxation. However, the number of areas appointed grew so large that the basic aims of the acts were obscured.

The Submission of the National
Comprehensive Land Development Plan
and its Implication in Physical Planning

The National Comprehensive Land Development Plan, which was to be the basic framework for land development, was completed in 1962, twelve years after its authorization act was enacted. Its aim was to plan for balanced development among the regions by preventing the overgrowth of cities and by lessening development gaps among regions.

In order to attain "balanced" development, a "base-area development" system was introduced. The "base areas" were large urban centers in the

developing regions chosen because they were rich in
locational potentialities, they showed high efficiency
in economic investment, and they generated wide
influence in the region.

In 1963, New Industrial Cities were chosen,
according to the New Industrial City Construction
Promotion Act (1962). These cities were to become
the foci of the base areas. The designation of these
locations, therefore, became a major political issue,
involving local political groups, which made active
moves to get their cities appointed. As a result,
the number of cities was increased to thirteen, with
six more semi-appointed ones, and the program became
far different from the one originally intended.
Within five years, it became apparent that the amount
of new public and private investment in these areas
was not as large as had been hoped.

Several points emerge in a review of the
policies and results of the postwar regional planning
administration. It is natural to expect that the
targets of regional planning will change, according
to the economic and social conditions in the
respective regions. In the immediate postwar times,
targets were set for resources development, especially
agriculture and hydroelectric power. In the last ten
years, the economy grew largely through private sector
activity in the advanced regions. Therefore, the aim
of regional planning has been directed largely toward
the welfare goal of eradicating the development gap
that the rapid economic growth has brought about.
This was a step forward for development planning,
but the policy has proved difficult to implement.

Saburo Okita states that:

If the planning is a resources development
type planning, it can insist on the
priority by the region to some extent.
If it is a national economic and central
planning, priority could be set against
the voice of the localities. However,
when the "eradication of the gap in the
development" becomes the main target,
all the localities would become the
object of the development planning, thus
resulting in all the people raising their
dissent. The basic reasons for the
present flood of local development plans
are here. This trouble cannot be done

away with unless a strong national
planning, aimed at remodelling Japan
into a new pattern of open economic
system, is set.[1]

Tokyo Metropolitan Regional Planning

Before World War II, Tokyo-Fu was a special
prefecture with a governor appointed by the central
government. It consisted of the City of Tokyo
(7 kilometers in radius) and several townships.
During the war period, the governor's power was
increased, and the City of Tokyo was amalgamated
into the Tokyo prefecture (15 kilometers radius from
the city center). After the war, urbanization
continued in the surrounding areas, and many cities
were developed privately around Tokyo. However, the
extent of the densely inhabited districts covered
the three prefectures adjoining Tokyo. The zone of
influence was still larger (some 40 kilometers in
radius). To cope with this large area, an intergovernmental agency (the National Capital Region
Redevelopment Commission) was established in 1950.
The main concern of the Commission was to restrict
Tokyo from excessive growth. In their planning,
they relied heavily on the Greater London Plan.
The Commission's Master Plan of 1958 covered an area
of 50 kilometers radius from the center of the city
and attempted to restrict the expansion of Tokyo to
within a theoretical "green belt" of 15 to 25
kilometers radius from the center, at the same
time creating satellite cities outside the green
belt to absorb the anticipated influx of population.

Very soon, however, the continued concentration
of population in Tokyo made it necessary to change
this Plan. The Plan was revised to cover an area of
100 kilometers in radius, and a new master plan is
being drawn up. The "green belt" idea has been
given up, and the region is divided into built-up
areas, inner suburban areas (50 kilometers radius
zone), and outer suburban areas. In recent years,
the infrastructure has been considerably improved
in the built-up areas through the construction of
trunk roads, freeways, subways, and railroad terminals.
In the suburban areas, Tama New Town (300,000 in
population and 30 kilometers west of Tokyo) and the
Research and University Town and the New International
Airport (both 70 kilometers from Tokyo) are scheduled
for construction. All are key projects of the
Master Plan of the Capital Region.

The same approach has been used in the Kinki
Region (Osaka-Kobe-Kyoto Region) and Chubu Region
(Nagoya Region), the other large agglomerations that
face the same kind of problems as Tokyo. Intergovernmental agencies for the Kinki Region and the
Chubu Region were created in 1964 and 1966,
respectively, and are now working on comprehensive
plans for the regions.

It is too early to judge the success of this
intergovernmental approach to regional planning, but
the recognition of the need for effectively linking
together the different levels of government is a
desirable development.

CITY PLANNING

Modern City Planning Until 1900

Feudal cities in Japan generally were built
around the central castles where feudal lords lived
and from which they controlled flourishing local
trades under their protection. Defense was the key
factor in the design of these castle towns. Usually
a network of narrow alleys covered the entire town.
Animal-drawn vehicles were the major mode of
transportation. Waterways carried most of the
goods and materials. These existing structures
found Japanese cities meeting the impact of modern
civilization with very obsolete urban patterns.

After the Meiji Revolution, the new government
tried to introduce a railway network throughout the
country. The construction of a modern road system
was delayed. Construction of ports, canals, and
bridges was required as new manufacturing industries
developed; improvement of the urban environment was
demanded as the location of factories created
nuisances in the surrounding neighborhoods and as
problems of public hygiene became recognized. In
response to these urban problems, the first city
planning measure was taken in Tokyo. The Tokyo
Municipal Ordinance was passed in 1888 in spite of
the strong opposition of the Senate, where the
interest of feudal landlords was still strong.
As the Ordinance was related to the improvement of
the capital city, the powers were given to the central
government. For example, the City Planning Commission
which was in charge of the preparation of plans, was
put under direct control of the Minister of Interior,

and the plans had to be approved by the Cabinet.
This pattern of planning organization, which was
adopted because it dealt with the planning of the
capital, prevailed in other cases as well and created
the centralized character of Japanese city planning.

Thus, city planning, although officially
established in Japan in 1888, was limited in
effectiveness because of poor financial support
until the period after World War I.

By the 1920's, Japan had advanced in her
industrialization, and rapid urbanization was taking
place. Expansion of the cities across traditional
boundaries was accelerated by the advent of
electric suburban railways.

In response to this situation, the Tokyo
Municipal Ordinance of 1888 was revised so that it
could be applied to other larger cities, including
Kyoto, Osaka, Yokohama, Kobe, and Nagoya.

The national City Planning Act, together with
the Urban Building Act as its sister law, was
enacted in 1919 and gave a solid foundation to city
planning practice and its administration. This Act
defined city planning as "planning concerning major
urban facilities covering urban areas which form,
or should form, socioeconomic units regardless of
administrative boundaries." This delineation of
planning areas was very significant from a technical
point of view. But, at the same time, it must be
noted that this Act consolidated the past planning
process with its centralized planning organization.[2]

Authorized planning areas were gradually
extended, and by 1933 all cities and some townships
and villages had been included under the control of
the Minister of Interior.

As a general standard in delineating planning
areas, a time distance of one hour from the central
business district was adopted. Taking transportation
capacity into account, the time distance was translated into a physical distance of 15 kilometers.
The Ministry of Interior tried to apply this standard,
but localities to which authorized city planning was
applied did not fully consent. As a result,
surrounding cities, townships, and villages in the
metropolitan areas tended to be excluded from the
planning areas of the central cities. Large urban

areas were divided into two or more planning areas
along the prefectural borders. The cities which had
acquired the status of independent city corporations
before they were included in one of the planning
areas wanted to have independent planning areas of
their own. Moreover, surrounding townships and
villages that once had belonged to a metropolitan
planning area tried to be independent when their
populations became large enough for them to acquire
the status of a city.

The major planning areas were decreasing as
they lost their fringe population to the newly
established city corporations. This tendency was in
conflict with the need for comprehensive metropolitan
planning. Efforts were made for the amalgamation of
fringe towns and villages to the central city, but
this was too difficult politically to be realized.
The problem remained unsolved until after World War II.

The Content of Official City Planning

City planning, as it was conceived in the
City Planning Act, included:

a) planning and execution of improvement of
public facilities, such as streets, bridges, ports,
parks, and utilities;

b) area-wide operation of development and
redevelopment projects by special legal means,
such as land readjustment or reallotment (later
referred to as land reallotment); and

c) zoning and other planning controls over
building.

Theoretically, the land use plan should precede
the planning of public facilities and land reallotment projects, which are tools for the implementation
of the plan. In Japan, however, because of rapid
urbanization, the planning process consisted of the
preparation of a rough sketch of future land use,
which served only for drawing street pattern maps and
for designating project areas of land reallotment
works. In this dynamic situation, it was impossible
to follow the normal procedure of land use planning
that was popular in the stabilized urban societies,
and zoning control was not exercised in the usual way.
Emphasis was put on a minimal exclusion of nuisances.
Proper land use control was severely handicapped by
this legal arrangement.

Land Reallotment Operation as a
Major Instrument of Official City Planning

Land reallotment has served as the major
instrument of official city planning since the
enactment of the City Planning Act in 1919.
In 1954, a special act for this process was created.
In Japan, suburban development commonly takes place
on intensively cultivated land, and subdivision
proceeds on the already established irregular
pattern of the farming units.

Jiro Tanaka describes this situation:

Even before 1919 when the City Planning
Act was enacted, readjustment of
agricultural land in the suburban areas
had been utilized for the preparation of
urbanization. It served, in the urban
fringe, not so much for the promotion
of efficient agricultural production by
means of rationalization of farming
units, but as the proceeding adjustment
of the urban development pattern for
the future subdivision. Once physical
boundaries of agricultural lands are
readjusted, accompanied with the
exchanges of their property rights,
and roads and drainages for farming are
improved, thus giving higher utility
for agricultural uses, it certainly
paves the way at the same time for a
better urban development pattern,
because as urbanized areas encroach,
agricultural lands are converted to
building sites, utilizing straightened
agricultural roads for streets and
farming drainages for urban uses, thus
realizing smooth, piecemeal conversion
of farming land to building sites on
the regular pattern.[3]

The land reallotment technique was used to
obtain land from the owners for dedication as streets
and parks. Improvement of the remaining land was to
serve as compensation to the owners for their loss
of land for dedication, thus enabling public agencies
to build public infrastructure with a minimum
expenditure.

Land reallotment was executed by voluntary associations of landowners. In the areas where administrative power was strong, the technique functioned well and demonstrated considerable achievements, especially on the urbanizing fringe areas. But in the inner cities, where rational redevelopment was demanded, it was very difficult to achieve land reallotment because building sites already had been subdivided into minute units with complex property rights. Therefore, redevelopment had to wait until natural disasters (such as typhoons, floods, or fires) provided the opportunity for reconstruction in a better urban pattern. Ironically, the Kanto earthquake in 1923 and the damage of World War II provided the best opportunity for the advancement of Japanese city planning.

Land reallotment was considered one of the basic measures of city planning and sometimes was misunderstood as a synonym for city planning. Unfortunately, it demanded a tremendously complex procedure, and as the land values of suburban areas came to rise without any improvement, it ceased to be attractive to the landowners.

The Change After the War-- "Democratization" of City Planning

The end of World War II provided new opportunities for city planning. The devastated cities needed drastic reconstruction works. Responding to the opportunity, city planners drew up many ambitious reconstruction plans.

The revision of the national constitution led to democratic changes in the governmental form and in the legal system. City planning was not an exception.

The degree of intervention of the central government was greatly reduced. After the enactment of the Local Government Act in 1948, the national and the local city planning commissions (through which the central government had controlled city planning practice in the past) were abolished, and new local planning boards were created. The former commissions had been staffed with privileged bureaucrats in the capacity of national public officials. But now local public officials, responsible to the elected governor, fulfilled the role of the secretariat of the new city planning commissions.

This change brought progress in the planning process as the opinions of local citizens were institutionally secured and reflected in the city planning.

Unfortunately, the change was sudden, occurring at the time when the massive war reconstruction operations started. As a result, there was a major shortage of technical skills, and many of the smaller municipalities had no technical experts. A lack of technical ability became one of the major bottlenecks in city planning.

Since the budget allocations for city planning implementation were restricted and the war-devastated cities were short of revenues, the ambitious plans could not be realized. More moderate plans with fewer planned improvements had to be adopted.

Throughout this period, a wide variety of construction works were needed. This need, in turn, led to competition between government agencies, reinforced by the enactment of new laws that regulated in detail the construction and the maintenance of public works. Each agency proceeded to make its own plans for its own projects.

The power of planning and execution was dissipated among the individual fields of public works. For example, jurisdiction of the public water surface was transferred to the Port and Harbor Bureau of the Ministry of Transportation and was put outside city planning control. Reclamation of land surrounding public water surfaces, including the busiest harbor areas (which became very popular as seafront industries developed), was planned and executed by that authority without serious cooperation with city planning authorities. Housing policy also was established independently and was separate from over-all city planning considerations.

Yoshitane Maeda describes this situation:

The period after the big change of city planning administration in 1948 seemed to me, in short, the era of competition (among execution bodies of each public works), seeking a larger share of the very scarce financial resources as the outcome of administrative reorganization.

I feel that before the war, powerful
central government could control
everything; before the war, the operations concerning the canals and waterways
in cities were executed by city planning
authorities. But after the war, the
execution agencies of the public works
were dissolved into various ministries,
such as the Ministry of Construction
and the Ministry of Transportation.
The public works that city planning
authorities could control were narrowly
restricted to the improvements of streets
and parks. This resulted in the commonly
felt very narrow view of city planning
authorities. The adjustment function
of a prefecture from the regional point
of view was frustrated, for it took a
very long time to consult with many
municipalities in the prefecture in the
process of preparation of the plans.[4]

Present Problems and Their Remedies

Rapid economic growth imposed serious problems
upon the infrastructure of Japanese cities. The
cities, which had developed without much motor
vehicle transportation, now were required to make
fundamental changes because of the impact of
motorization. Dispersion of population toward the
suburbs created new transportation demands by
commuters to central cities. In order to serve the
expanding population around metropolitan cities, a
tremendous volume of water was needed, and regional
policies for securing water resources were needed.
Provision of sewerage, which had long been neglected,
became a pressing problem. Improvement of river
control in cities was necessary because large-scale
land use changes from agriculture to urban uses
caused an increase in water volume. Growing public
nuisances from the developing industries were
threatening the lives of the urban inhabitants.
Housing problems were serious. Uncontrolled urban
sprawl was destroying open spaces for recreation.

Confronted with these problems, the city
governments took several measures. New semipublic
development corporations were established in Tokyo
and Osaka for improvement of urban streets through
a network of toll expressways superimposed upon the
existing street pattern. The improved railway

systems for commuters in major Japanese cities were
formed by a combination of elevated railways (run by
the National Railway) and suburban railways (run by
private companies), linked at central terminals.
In the case of Tokyo, the construction and service
of underground railways was carried on by a unique
public corporation. The creation of a comprehensive
urban railway system--by the cooperation of the
Ministry of Construction, the Ministry of Transportation, and municipal planning authorities--was one
of the major achievements of recent Japanese city
planning.

Development of subcenters at the transportation
nodes has been undertaken through new public
corporations, such as the Shinjuku subcenter in Tokyo.

Thus, the tendency is for large-scale urban
development operations to be carried out by
independent agencies. This is quite efficient from
the point of view of project execution, but it
requires complicated planning activities to put
these operations under unified control.

Several measures have been taken for more
reasonable acquisition of land for public uses.
The price of land in Japanese cities, in comparison
with those in American and European cities, is
astonishingly high. This phenomenon may be
attributable to the combined effect of the
specially tenacious inclination toward land-
ownership by the people (who have preserved the
social characteristics of an agricultural nation)
and to the general support for protection of private
property (which has been brought forth by the sudden
democratization of Japan).

Land policy is a major problem in Japan's
development. Some remedies are under consideration
in the government, especially in the Ministry of
Construction. One measure envisions the improvement
of condemnation procedures through the Compulsory
Land Acquisition Act, and another calls for intensification of land use control in the National City
Planning Act. The key issue is the time at which the
land price should be determined in the procedure of
compulsory acquisition: at the time of the planning
decision to acquire it or at the sanction of the
operation by the superior authority? In practice,
condemnation power has rarely been exercised, and
purchase is usually made at the full market price
that includes its development value.

Implementation of city planning in Japan is largely dependent upon the land reallotment technique that preserves property ownership on or near the original site. But it is extremely difficult to apply this method in the built-up urban areas. In these areas, over-all compulsory purchase is preferred to the land reallotment method. As a result, an interesting idea concerning compensation in redevelopment operation has been evolved.

The idea of compensation in kind through relocation of property is so deeply rooted in Japan that it was adopted in the Act of Urban Redevelopment Concerning Improvement of Public Facilities enacted in 1961. The land that is acquired is to be compensated for with floor space in a building that will be built on the site where the original land is located. This idea is incorporated in the Urban Redevelopment Act, which is now under discussion in the National Diet. This Act will provide that the redevelopment operation can be organized if two thirds of the property owners or leaseholders agree upon it and form an association for it, and that those interested parties are compensated by the floor space of the building on the redeveloped site in proportion to their share of the original land, through the legal procedure of so-called vertical transference of property.

The redevelopment operation of Shinbashi (a subcenter of Tokyo), which included expansion of the square in front of the National Railway Station, was executed according to this method. It created a park square and accommodated most of the commercial activities located in the area in two modern buildings constructed on the site.

HOUSING PLANNING

Development of Housing Policies

The first government action for housing on a large scale was taken during the reconstruction of Tokyo after the earthquake in 1923. Dojunkai, a nonprofit organization, was established by the government at that time to make housing available to the people in need. There was a war-time housing program for drafted industrial workers in 1941, and Dojunkai was reorganized into Jutaku-Eidan, a semi-governmental organization for housing construction

and management. Thus, public housing in Japan
started as emergency countermeasures against major
disasters or emergencies.

Slum clearance was also a problem, and, in 1927,
the Slum Clearance Act was enacted. There was little
achievement in this field, however, until after World
War II. During this period, the accumulation of
capital to cope with the rapid growth of industry was
so urgent in Japan that the housing sector was
neglected.

The tremendous housing demand after World War II
and the short supply were really the forces that
promoted the formation of public housing policy.
The government's responsibility in housing has now
been recognized.

The general policy for public housing was
formulated and grew into a subsidized public housing
program executed by local authorities. Subsidized
public housing serves the low- and lowest-income
people, with a 50-80 per cent subsidy on the cost
of construction. The construction itself was
authorized by the Public Housing Act of 1951.

The Japan Housing Loan Corporation (JHLC) was
established in 1950 to extend long-term, low-interest
loans for owner-occupied housing. And, in 1955, the
Japan Housing Corporation (JHC) was established with
the multiple aims of supplying rental housing,
providing for long-term installment sales of apartment houses, and developing large tracts as new towns
in the urban regions--where the housing shortage was
acute. These provisions became the three main
vehicles of Japanese housing policy.

Public housing construction now contributes
one third of the annual volume of housing construction
in Japan, of which JHLC supports about half.

Several characteristics of housing policy have
emerged from the postwar developments. First, the
tremendous housing shortage has committed the
government to meet the quantitative need. This. is
one of the reasons why the size of dwelling units
has been kept small. Public housing started from
the emergency housing standard of 20 square meters
per unit. Even now, public housing averages only
40 square meters per unit.

Second, there is a strong desire to construct
incombustible houses, influenced no doubt by the
fact that Japanese cities of "wood and paper" have
been destroyed repeatedly by disasters.

Third, there has been a strong interest in
constructing large housing groups or communities.
In the past, the Japanese had little understanding
of "community" in the modern sense. Apartment house
living was quite unfamiliar to them, but mass
construction has been achieved through the creation
of a number of big communities of multistoried
apartment houses.

These underlying characteristics of the housing
programs have raised many problems in urban planning,
while at the same time stimulating its development.
The experience of JHC serves to illustrate these
points.

The Activities of the
Japan Housing Corporation (JHC)

The reason for picking JHC as a case study of
the three major Japanese housing agencies is its
role as a pioneer in establishing the position of
housing policy in urban planning. Its achievements
are as follows:

a) The subsidized housing program of the local
authorities stressed social welfare. The JHC, on
the other hand, emphasized the rotation of capital
and the introduction of private capital for housing
construction. The higher interest rate required by
private capital was reduced by a capital grant from
the government.

However, as the grant was limited, it was
necessary to charge higher rentals than the more
fully subsidized public housing. Accordingly, JHC
housing was, from the beginning, a program for
middle-income families. This meant, however, that
it was diverted from the basic objective of public
housing: to provide low-rent housing for low-income
families.

b) Even though metropolitan regions expanded
over existing administrative boundaries, the public
housing supplied by the local authorities was limited
to areas within each particular jurisdiction. JHC
was created to overcome this problem by developing

housing over the whole metropolitan region, regardless
of existing administrative boundaries. This was
necessary to alleviate the metropolitan problem, but
it led the JHC into conflicts with the self-governing
principle of local authorities.

c) Apartment house living was quite unfamiliar
to the Japanese citizens, and many problems were
created by the occupation of buildings by persons
unfamiliar with urban living patterns.

d) New developments were located further and
further away from the urban centers because of easy
land acquisition and low cost, and the size of the
developments became larger and larger. The isolated
location made the provision of community facilities
imperative. And for providing better community
facilities, the size of the development had to be
larger. Thus, decentralization and enlargement of
the scale of the housing developments proceeded hand
in hand, and many self-contained communities were
created in distant suburbs.

However, these large developments also created
a demand for other social overhead investments, such
as traffic systems, regional water supply, and
sewage. Generally, in suburban areas the standard
of public facilities and services was low, and the
fiscal capabilities of local governments were too
limited to cope with the new demands. As a result,
local governments did not favor JHC's developments,
which frequently burdened the cities with new
financial responsibilities.

e) JHC also was expected to construct new towns
in the implementation of the plan proposed by the
National Capital Region Redevelopment Commission.
In this program, land acquisition was done by means
of purchase and land reallotment. The lands were
utilized for public facilities, for JHC rental
housing projects, and for housing lots to be sold by
JHC (in the case of land for sale, the houses had
to be built within two years of the purchase). The
rest was reallocated to former landlords. Here,
again, it was realized that the initial settlement
invited further newcomers and accelerated the
effective use of the overhead investments. These
new town developments have proved their effectiveness
but suffer from the same problem as the apartment
housing developments regarding the additional

financial burdens imposed on local authorities.
Measures are now being taken by JHC to share the
costs of social overhead.

The progress and problems discussed above show
that the development of residential areas and the
construction of new towns must be carried out in
close relation to regional planning, and with
sufficient provision for local finance.

In 1963, the New Residential Town Development
Act was enacted to foster the construction of new
residential towns. This Act stipulates that local
governments or JHC are authorized to develop large
tracts and to construct infrastructures and public
facilities in order to create new residential towns.
It also includes provisions for land acquisition.
Based on this Act, new town projects of a larger
scale--such as Tama New Town (300,000 in population)
and Research and University Town (100,000 in population), both outside of Tokyo--are now in progress,
along with the Kita-Osaka New Town project of
200,000 population (promoted by the Osaka prefectural
government) and the JHC's new town projects.

Private Housing

Public housing has developed rapidly, but its
total is still only one third of annual housing
construction. The rest is private housing, without
any governmental assistance, on a low standard,
especially in the rental housing field. Rental
housing amounted to 11.3 per cent of the total supply
in 1950 and increased to 34.4 per cent in 1960. The
standard of owner-occupied housing has gradually
improved, but not that of rental housing. The
average floor area of rental housing is approximately
30 square meters. Since 1960, construction of wooden
tenements of an extremely low standard has increased,
especially inside and on the fringes of large cities.

The Japanese housing supply for low- and middle-
income classes now consists of a) public housing of
a reasonable standard (still not high) far from the
city center and b) the private tenements of low
standard inside the city center. In this situation,
blue-collar workers who cannot afford to commute long
distances are obliged to live inside the city in
low-standard housing at high rent. This is a
serious urban problem.

There is no housing code act in Japan, so the
Building Standard Act provides the only legal control
over public housing. However, its main provisions are
in the form of structural standards, and it is unable
to restrict low-standard housing. So far, urban
planning and housing policy in Japan have had little
success in improving the residential environment of
the private sector.

Urban Redevelopment

There are two major objectives to urban
redevelopment through housing policy in Japan:
a) slum clearance and b) efficiency in land use,
coupled with disaster prevention.

Slum Clearance

Slum clearance projects in Japan started in
1927, but little was accomplished until after 1960.
Even now, their annual construction is only about
5,000 houses, representing only a minor part of total
housing construction. The principles of the program
are:

a) Displaced households are to be relocated
in the same project area.

b) The local government undertakes the project
with compulsory power of expropriation and takes
charge of the management of the dwellings as rental
public housing after completion.

c) The size of a project can be as small as
0.15 hectare and/or more than fifty dwellings.

These principles for slum clearance limit its
flexibility in practice and hinder the further
expansion of the program. Rights of ownership and
leasehold on properties are so fragmented and
complicated in the slum areas that their reorganization always involves great difficulties. Moreover,
projects are so small in scale that they rarely show
enough tangible benefits to justify the effort.

Efficiency in Land Use,
Coupled with Disaster Prevention

There exists a strong desire in Japan to make
cities incombustible. The Disaster-Prevention Block
Construction Act provides government assistance[5]

in planning an association of building owners of
designated districts for developing a complete area
of incombustible structures. Since project areas
were often located in the commercial districts of
urban areas, this program was effective in guiding
private business into urban renewal activities.
Combined with other public measures, such as JHLC
loans, it has obtained good results.

Measures have also been taken to make use of
"air rights" in order to secure more available floor
space for housing above existing buildings. This
same idea was included in the Urban Area Redevelopment Act, except that the former focuses on housing
space, whereas the latter includes urban public
facilities.

Construction of housing units above existing
buildings has been carried out since the late 1950's
as part of the JHC rental housing program and JHLC-
financed private housing program. JHC makes an
agreement with the landlord to construct its rental
housing above the shops and/or offices. JHC then
constructs and sells the units on a long-term basis
to the landlord. The rent of the land is paid to
the landlord. This measure has been successful and
suggests a new technique for urban redevelopment
that may be applicable elsewhere.

Another redevelopment opportunity has been
created by the shift of factories from inside the
city to the suburban areas. The vacant lots left
behind provide a good chance for redevelopment.
The Urban Land Acquisition Fund has been provided
in Tokyo to enable the local authorities to acquire
such lots. This has meant a shift in direction from
the utilization of "air rights" to the construction
of large-scale urban residential complexes with the
over-all purchase of the land.

This, however, does not necessarily mean a
bright prospect for the future of urban redevelopment.
The land cost imposes a great burden upon the housing
and, as a result, housing costs tend to be high.
The floor space index and the population density of
the present projects have already reached 200 per
cent and 700 persons per hectare, respectively.
Moreover, mainly because of the land cost, the rent
is higher than that of surrounding housing.
Consequently, redevelopment housing is available
only to higher-income families. The environment of

these former factory sites usually is not of high
residential quality. We cannot conclude, as yet,
what kind of social class will adopt to such projects
and what kind of impact such a big group of high-
density dwellings will produce in nearby neighborhoods.
Housing of this type by JHC amounts to 7,000 units
this year, exceeding that of the slum-clearance
projects.

Evaluation of Public Housing in Japan

Japan's housing policy has not been totally
satisfactory from the point of view of city planning.
However, housing--especially in the public sector--
has grown in scale to cover a full range of urban
functions. It has been proved that public housing
is an efficient tool in implementing city planning,
one which is gaining momentum as the amount of
construction is increasing.

Perhaps it is time to realize that the
construction of infrastructure alone does not
constitute full implementation of city planning.
In Japan, now, tools are available to cope with
this problem, and integrated planning covering a wide
range of physical and social factors should be
considered.

CONCLUSION

From this brief review of urban planning
administration at various levels of government, it
can be seen that policies were developed in response
to the necessities of the times, with various piecemeal approaches--inevitable in Japan during the period
of poor capital accumulation, weak administrative
power, extremely rapid growth, and concentration of
urban population. In other words, planning
administration in Japan was shaped in the process
of coping with pressing requirements, thus producing
the present urban agglomeration.

Japan now is in a different stage of development.
The impact of agglomeration continues to increase,
but the power to cope with it is now available.
Japan is at a new starting point. It is time to
strengthen the planning system and its administration.
The country needs a more flexible and dynamic approach
and, at the same time, a wider and deeper insight into
the problems of a massive urban society. It is of

critical importance now that planning at each level
be integrated. In the past, planning in Japan was
performed with different objectives and principles
at each level--national, regional, city, and
community. However, although planning is realized
through separate projects, these projects are bound
to create a total physical result and serve human
society as an entity. There must be a consistency
in each of them. Now that the elements of human
activity are becoming more and more closely related
and the extent of activities is becoming wider, this
consistency is much more necessary than it was when
activities were relatively isolated and limited.

It is hoped that this examination of the
Japanese experience will provide some assistance
to the countries that are now undergoing similar
processes of development.

NOTES TO CHAPTER 3

1. Kiyoshi Tsuchiya and Saburo Okita, et al.,
The Japanese Regional Planning (Tokyo: Diamond-
Sha, 1965), pp. 48-49.

2. According to this Act, plans and projects
of improvement should be referred to the City
Planning Commission and then should be filed for
the adoption of the Minister of Interior. After
this, they would be sent for the approval of the
Cabinet. The City Planning Commission was the
advisory body under the Minister of Interior,
consisting of the Central Commission and the Local
Commissions. The former was set up in the Ministry
of Interior and was headed by the Minister himself.
The latter were located in the municipalities where
legally defined city planning was practiced.
However, they were presided over by the governor
of the prefecture to which the municipalities
belonged, who was appointed by the central government. The mayors and some of the members of the
municipal councils could participate in the
Commissions, while the municipal councils themselves
were not allowed to take any part in the planning
process. Actually, local planning commissions were
located in the prefectural offices, and although
their permanent staffs were paid from the prefectural
treasury, they had the status of public officials
belonging to the national government.

3.   Jiro Tanaka, et al., New Town Planning.
A report of discussion by experts in which
Kichiemon Kawana and Yoshitane Maeda took part.
(Tokyo: Hyoron-Sha, 1966), p. 26.

4.   Yoshitane Maeda.   Ibid., p. 48.

5.   The extent of assistance is as follows:
project planning cost, architectural design cost,
soil survey cost, building removal cost, common
facilities equipment cost, and temporary shop
construction cost.

CHAPTER **4** THE HOUSING THRESHOLD
FOR
LOWEST-INCOME GROUPS:
THE CASE OF INDIA

Alfred P. Van Huyck*

INTRODUCTION

The housing problem in the developing countries
has been a source of constant concern to administrators, architects, sociologists, economists, engineers,
and planners. Those who are charged with guiding the
future of the developing countries all agree that
housing is a problem that has so far escaped solution
and, in fact, is recognized as growing every year.

There is, of course, argument over the extent
of the problem, the definitions used to describe it,
and the validity of the statistics, but there is no
disagreement about the argument that the problem
exists at a vast magnitude. The real argument begins
when the experts turn their attentions to the question
of what to do about it. Here, they polarize into a
variety of strongly defended positions. Leland Burns

---

*Alfred P. Van Huyck, B.A., M.R.P., is President
of PADCO, Inc. All references to Calcutta are based
on the author's experience as Chief Planner, Urban
Renewal for The Ford Foundation Planning Advisory
Group in Calcutta. PADCO was in no way involved in
this work. Credit for various aspects should be
given to the members of the Calcutta Metropolitan
Planning Organisation and The Ford Foundation Planning Advisory Group. Of course, the conclusions
drawn are the sole responsibility of the author and
do not necessarily reflect the opinions of the
agencies involved.

identified four main positions that have been taken
in public policy on housing, vis-à-vis alternative
investments:

1. Investment should be concentrated in
    heavy industry and agriculture, to
    the virtual exclusion of social
    overhead projects such as housing
    programs.

2. A fixed share of new investment in
    plant and equipment should be earmarked
    for housing as a necessary adjunct to
    industrial development.

3. Housing is justified, along with
    alternative investments, for its
    contribution to economic development.

4. A sizable share of capital formed
    should be set aside for residential
    construction since housing is
    necessary for social and political
    stability and progress.[1]

Various programs that have been tried in the
developing countries have taken various approaches
based on one or another of these policy positions,
but still there is no concensus. The reason is
obvious--there is merit to all the points, and,
therefore, individuals react as their own hearts
and minds dictate.

In this chapter, I propose to explore the
middle ground by suggesting that it is possible to
obtain the rapid and dramatic improvement in the
standard of living sought by the socially concerned
while at the same time recognizing the tight
constraints imposed by the economist. The hypothesis hinges on the breakthrough created by no longer
thinking of the housing problem in terms of the
housing unit but, rather, in terms of the total
environment in which the individual lives.

I suggest that there is a housing threshold:
a point along the income distribution curve below
which it is not possible to provide housing, either
publicly or privately, on a massive scale commensurate
with the needs at any reasonable set of "minimum"
standards. The housing threshold may fluctuate
somewhat between urban areas and, certainly,

between urban and rural areas. But, at some point, the mass of low-income people to be served, the costs of housing in any form, the administrative mechanism required, and the shortage of permanent building materials combine to establish the lower limit below which standard housing cannot be made available to the people on a widespread basis.

If the concept of a housing threshold is recognized in the development of a total program for housing, it will be possible to maximize the amount of return from the investment of a housing dollar by concentrating on environmental improvement programs for the lowest-income groups and establishing the mechanisms such as savings institutions, housing cooperatives, self-help housing, and other such programs for those who can be assisted, at reasonable cost, to cross the housing threshold. Subsidized housing programs, more the equivalent of public housing now being built in many countries in the world, become practical only for those people still higher on the income curve--but still not yet prepared to command standard housing in the private market.

Many experts in the housing field in the developing countries, such as John Turner of Massachusetts Institute of Technology and Charles Abrams of Columbia University, have recognized the futility of conventional housing solutions in the developing countries.

Charles Abrams expressed it well when he wrote:

> It is manifest therefore that all
> prevailing ideas of wholesale slum
> clearance and building of costly housing
> must be abandoned, and that some fresh
> thinking must be brought to bear on the
> shelter problem. The provision of the bare
> essentials may have to be the world's sad
> but only reasonable alternative. Once we
> understand the enormity of the problem,
> however, there may be ways of dealing with
> it. It is only when hope is given up and
> eyes are closed to reality that crisis
> becomes inevitable.[2]

The hypothesis that I put forth here is largely an extension of a line of thinking already well

developed but not yet generally accepted. The
opposing position was strongly stated in an
editorial in a planning journal in India:

> The basic standards in housing and
> planning are arrived at not only from
> considerations of cost but also from
> considerations of creating the desirable
> sociological and physical environment
> necessary for the healthy growth of the
> individuals and the community. Such
> standards have been established by
> various committees and technical missions.
> The Environmental Hygiene Committee
> recommended a two-room house as the
> minimum for a family. The U.N. Technical
> Mission on Housing, the later Seminar and
> Conference on Housing and Town Planning,
> and other reports published by national
> and international agencies concerned
> with housing and town planning all
> recommend the two-room house with
> adequate sanitary and other facilities
> as the barest minimum if the normal
> aspirations of healthy living are to
> be achieved. . . .

> These standards cannot be lowered, what-
> ever be the community, whatever be its
> location, and whatever be the economic
> situation in the country. Substandard
> housing is but a step towards slums.
> Deliberate substandard housing will
> defeat the very purpose of housing as
> it will lead to the creation of future
> slums; the basic standards must be
> adhered to at all costs.[3]

The concept of a housing threshold is an effort
to bridge the philosophic gap between these positions--
accepting the economic realities but retaining central
social goals. In the remaining portions of this
chapter, I will try to describe the kinds of environmental programs that fall below the housing threshold
and the reasons these kinds of programs offer the
best hope for the substantial increase in the
standard of living that all desire.

THE HOUSING GAP

The housing problem in India, simply stated,
revolves around three basic problem factors:
population, low incomes, and the inadequacy of
present housing programs, public or private.

Population

Even though urbanization is not occurring at an
unusually fast rate in India, the total population
figures are still extremely high. Within the urban
areas, natural increase is taking place at between
1.5-2.0 per cent per year, which on top of the
80 million 1961 urban population means approximately
40 million births during the next twenty-five years,
at a time when the death rate is declining.
Migration will add millions more.

TABLE 1

POPULATION GROWTH AND PROJECTIONS
FOR INDIA, 1921-76

Year	India Population (million)	Per Cent Urban in India
1921	251	11.4
1931	279	12.1
1941	319	13.9
1951	361	17.3
1961	439	18.0
Projections	I	II
1966	492	18.1
1971	555	18.7
1976	625	19.3

Source: For Projections I, 1961 Study Group of
         the Planning Commission (Third Five-Year
         Plan--Notes on Population and Employment,
         Table 1, Column 4, p. 750).

         For Projections II, estimated urbanization
         rate of logistic curve.

The eleven largest cities of India contain 21.5
million people, or approximately one fourth the total
urban population. Still, these largest urban centers
are growing most rapidly.

TABLE 2

POPULATION GROWTH OF MAJOR METROPOLITAN
CITIES IN INDIA DURING 1931-61

Name of City	Population 1931	1941	(add 000) 1951	1961	Varia- tion 1931-61
Calcutta Metropolitan District	2,485	4,054	5,253	6,575	4,090
Greater Bombay	1,303	1,695	2,839	4,152	2,849
Madras	647	777	146	1,729	1,082
Delhi	447	696	1,437	2,344	1,897
Hyderabad	667	739	1,086	1,251	784
Ahmedabad	314	607	828	1,206	892
Bangalore	311	411	786	1,207	896
Kanpuz	244	487	708	971	727
Poona	263	350	600	737	474
Lucknow	275	387	497	656	381
Nagpur	242	329	485	690	448

Source: Census of India, 1931-61 and Government
          of India, Ministry of Health, Town and
          Country Planning Organisation, "Population
          Growth and Urban and Regional Planning -
          A Background Paper Contributed to the Asia
          Population Conference: 1963."

Low Incomes

Besides the sheer magnitude of the urban population, there is the severe complication of low incomes for the vast majority of the people. Table 3 illustrates this problem clearly. Even allowing for the estimated improvement of income over the last six years, it is still obvious that at least 60 per cent of the households in urban India earn less than Rs. 2,000 per year, and probably 25 per cent of the households earn less than Rs. 1,000 annually.[4] If it is assumed that households at these income levels cannot afford more than 15 per cent of their income for rent, then monthly rentals of more than $2.00 per month cannot be paid by 50 per cent of the urban households, and 25 per cent cannot pay more than $1.50 per month. This low capacity to pay rent precludes these families from utilizing the present Government of India schemes, regardless of the amount of subsidy or the attractiveness of the projects, with the exception of the "open plot scheme."

Public Housing Programs

Against the background of such a massive population to be served and the extremely low incomes available, it is not surprising that the public housing program has been totally inadequate in dealing with the problem. Nonetheless, there has been a public housing program in India since 1952.

Expenditures on housing have increased in each Five-Year Plan, from an initial Rs. 33.5 crores[5] in the First Plan to a proposed Rs. 250 crores in the Fourth Plan. The percentage of the total Plan funds has, however, stayed a relatively constant 1.7 per cent. The Government of India's housing program has consisted of housing for government employees and what might be called social housing schemes, the latter consisting of a variety of programs designed to make housing available for people of low and middle income by a combination of loans and grants.

The total funds available for the different schemes are allotted to the states by the Planning Commission for each Plan period. The fund is finally given to the state against individual projects, and the Centre exercises detailed control in implementing even individual projects. For example, the state

government cannot transfer funds allotted for one
sanctioned project to another sanctioned project
under the same scheme without the explicit permission
of the Centre.

These programs rely on subsidies of between
60-75 per cent of the economic rent for each housing
unit. The problem of the massive subsidies required
to rehouse slum families was graphically presented
in a paper by Stanislaw H. Wellisz.[6] Using figures
of the average income of a slum family, he concluded,
after analysis, that the subsidy required to rehouse
one slum family amounts to Rs. 680 per year for a
sixty-year period, equal to the assumed life of the
structure, which means a total subsidy of $700 million
to rehouse just the present slum families of Calcutta
alone.

Even more interesting was Wellisz's conclusion
about who pays the cost of this subsidy. He concludes
that, because of indirect taxes, the burden falls
largely on the poorest families. Over one half the
subsidy for this type of housing comes from families
with monthly incomes of $20.00 or less. In short,
the poorest families are called upon to pay the
burden of rehousing the fortunate few who live in
the public housing projects.

There is a need for a total rethinking, leading
to a reorganization of the over-all role of government
in housing. More emphasis is required on establishing
procedures of private financing so that families with
steady income streams can build housing outside of
the government programs. There is a need to improve
the designs and construction techniques to conserve
scarce materials, rewrite the building codes,
introduce a constructive tax policy, establish
viable savings institutions, and increase the
density of new residential areas within the urban
centers. All of these things, as vital as they are,
still will not lead to the solution of the problem
of housing the lowest-income groups. There can be
no solution for this group until there is a realistic
understanding of the problem factors of population
and per capita income.

The present Government of India public housing
provision falls mainly under four schemes. The most
money has been sanctioned for the Industrial Housing
Scheme, where the maximum allowable rent is Rs. 36
per month, and the income limitation is set at

TABLE 3

INCOME PER HOUSEHOLD PER EARNER AND
SHARE IN THE AGGREGATE INCOME OF
DIFFERENT INCOME CLASSES (URBAN INDIA, 1960)

No.	Income Class (Income Before Tax) (Rs.)	Weighted Per Cent of Households*
	1	2
1.	Under 500	13.6
2.	500-999	28.9
3.	1,000-1,999	32.5
4.	2,000-2,999	10.6
5.	3,000-3,999	5.6
6.	4,000-4,999	3.1
7.	5,000-5,999	1.7
8.	6,000-7,999	1.7
9.	8,000-9,999	0.7
10.	10,000-14,999	0.8
11.	15,000-24,999	0.5
12.	25,000 or over	0.3
13.	All Classes	100.0

*Denotes the estimated per cent of households in
urban India covered by the survey. It may be noted
that the survey covered households (and household
population) in towns with a population of 10,000 or
more according to the 1951 Census, excluding Delhi.
The non-household population in these towns (such
as institutional population, beggars, and pavement
dwellers) was omitted from the purview of the study.
The survey results are estimated to be representative
of 12.1 million urban households.

Average Number of Earners per Household	Average Disposable Income per Household (Rs.)	Average Size of Household	Number of Inter-views**
3	4	5	6
1.1	300	3.0	466
1.4	753	4.2	1,028
1.5	1,390	5.1	1,194
1.7	2,387	6.3	473
1.7	3,476	6.6	273
1.6	4,487	6.4	196
1.9	5,438	7.7	141
1.9	6,706	7.3	173
1.9	8,674	7.3	95
2.0	12,292	7.8	155
2.0	18,867	8.4	100
1.7	40,452	7.2	87
1.5	1,862	5.0	4,381

**Denotes the number of interviews on which estimates are based. Source: "Urban Income and Saving," National Council of Applied Economic Research, Delhi (1962).

Source: India, Government of West Bengal, "A Proposal for a Low-Cost Temporary Urban Settlements Programme" (unpublished paper, Calcutta Metropolitan Planning Organisation, January, 1967), p. 21.

Rs. 4,200 per year. An almost equal amount of money
has been sanctioned for the Low-Income Housing
Scheme, where the rent is generally set at Rs. 27
per month, and the maximum allowable annual income
of a tenant family is Rs. 6,000. The Slum Clearance
and Economically Weaker Section Housing Scheme has
had less investment but serves families with a
maximum income of Rs. 3,000 per year, with maximum
allowable rents around Rs. 25 per month. Finally,
the Middle-Income Housing Scheme, which is essentially
on a loan basis, serves people in the income range of
Rs. 6,000-Rs. 15,000 per year.

Accepting the maximum allowable annual income
at the ceiling of the income groups served and
establishing a floor by assuming that a family can
afford 15 per cent of their annual income as rent,
it is possible to distribute the percentage of funds
sanctioned for housing among the income distribution
of urban households. When this curve is compared
to the curve of income distribution of urban households (see Graph 1), it can be readily seen that the
bulk of public investment in housing is made to
benefit the upper 25 per cent of the income groups
of the country. For most of the lower 75 per cent
of urban households, there is no benefit whatsoever.
Naturally, there are isolated cases where families
with less than Rs. 2,000 income per year are
sheltered in some of the complete projects, but
these are really exceptions that prove the rule.

It should be noted that even though the full
investment of housing funds is assigned to the
population with incomes of between Rs. 2,000-
Rs. 15,000, this still is far short of the total
need for housing in these income groups. But, this
is incidental to the main point of the graph, which
is to underscore the need for a new housing program
that will be directed toward the lowest-income
people in urban India.

It will take a careful research study to
determine where the housing threshold falls on the
income curve in urban India, but there can be no
doubt that it exists, probably in the range of
Rs. 2,500-Rs. 3,000. Any attempt to provide
standard housing below that level is doomed to
failure. There still should be a considerable
improvement in the methods and techniques of making
housing available to people above the housing
threshold, but there is a desperate need for new
thinking about the kinds of programs that can be
provided for people whose income falls below it.

GRAPH I

THE PUBLIC SECTOR HOUSING GAP

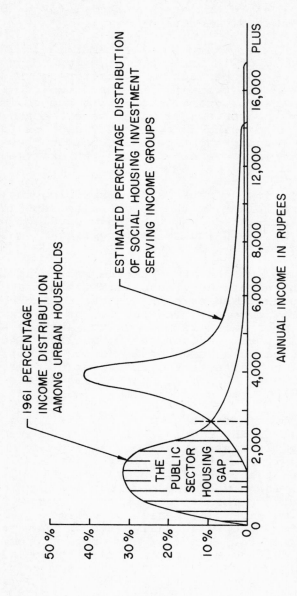

Source: India, Government of West Bengal, "A Proposal for a Low-Cost
Temporary Urban Settlements Programme," unpublished document
by Calcutta Metropolitan Planning Organisation, January 8, 1967.

THE CALCUTTA EXAMPLE OF THE HOUSING PROBLEM

Using generalized figures from all India is
proof enough of the totality of the housing problem,
but to look at Calcutta is to translate the problem
into its basic elements.

Almost every kind of urban amenity is lacking,
either wholly or in part, in the city. Huge
deficiencies in open space, education, garbage
collection, mass transit, and road construction
await workable programs, along with the environmental health problems of water sewerage and drainage.
It is not surprising that the city also is faced with
a chronic housing shortage and great problems of
dilapidation and overcrowding in the existing housing
supply.

The following paragraphs describing the present
housing conditions in the Calcutta Metropolitan Area
have been extracted from the Basic Development Plan
published by the Calcutta Metropolitan Planning
Organisation:

Housing in fact presents the most graphic
portrayal of the crisis of Metropolitan
Calcutta. The existing shortage in the
area is immense. The quality of housing
that does exist is poor on the average and
at its worst indescribably squalid. Shelter
is so basic a human need and its condition
so deeply affects the character of everyday
life, that this must be regarded as one of
the most tragic of the CMD's current deficits.

As shown in Table 4, of the 6.7 million
people in the CMD in 1961, 366,000 were
housed in institutions of one type or
another (hospitals, colleges, jails, etc.).
At least another 30,000 had no housing at
all. These were the pavement dwellers of
Calcutta. This figure is certainly on
the low side of a series of estimates of
how many people actually live on the streets
in Calcutta. The real number is extremely
difficult to measure, fluctuating greatly
with the seasons; but the existence of
this group is obviously a fact of life in
the city and its suburbs. Their miserable
plight is evident throughout the central
city areas, and requires no elaboration.

TABLE 4

POPULATION AND HOUSING SUPPLY, CMD, 1961

	Calcutta	Other CMD	CMD Rural	Total CMD
POPULATION (in thousands)				
Total Population	2,927	3,065	729	6,721
Housed in Institutions	274	82	10	366
Houseless	18	5	7	30
Household Population	2,635	2,978	712	6,325
HOUSING SUPPLY (including kutchha huts) (in thousands)				
Occupied Housing Units[a]	584	592	153	1,329
Occupied Rooms*	942	932	239	2,113
Average Rooms per Unit*	1.61	1.57	1.28	1.55
Vacant Units	25	27	8	60
OVERCROWDING AND CONDITION				
Household Population per Unit	4.51	5.03	4.65	4.76
Household Population per Room*	2.80	3.20	2.98	2.99
Units with Permanent Walls (thousands)*[b]	437	387	79	903
Per Cent of Units with Nonpermanent Walls*[b]	25.2	34.6	57.8	33.8

Note: *Starred items are estimates based on sample Census
       data for the CMD.

   a. A Housing Unit is defined here as a "Census
       House" used partly or wholly for dwelling purposes.

   b. Permanent walls are interpreted as walls made of
       concrete, cement, stone, or burnt brick only.

Source: Census of India, 1961, Vol. XVI, Part II-A and Part
         IV(i) and India, Government of West Bengal, Calcutta
         Metropolitan Planning Organisation, Basic Development
         Plan for the Calcutta Metropolitan District, 1966-1986
         (Calcutta: Public Relations Officer, Calcutta
         Metropolitan Planning Organisation, 1966), p. 27.

The remaining 6,325,000 were in the 1961
'household population'--people residing in
some form of non-institutional shelter.
Altogether, they occupied 1,329,000 housing
units, providing, on an average, one unit
for every 4.76 persons. This ratio itself
is not particularly high. The real problems
of the existing housing supply arise from
two other factors. First, most of the
units are extremely small in relation to
the number of people who are forced to live
in them. Second, the majority are in a
squalid condition with few of the physical
amenities of decent homes.

The first point implies overcrowding of
remarkable proportions. This can be
illustrated by two simple facts: (a) in
1961, the average CMD housing unit size
was only 1.55 rooms; the average occupancy
rate was 2.99 persons per room; (b) it has
been estimated that 77 per cent of all
Calcutta families in 1957 had less than
40 square feet of living space per person.

Averages even as low as these tend to
understate the problem. The distribution
of housing space is similar to that of
income: a relatively small minority at the
top have a disproportionately large share.
This means that the majority are living at
standards far below 40 square feet per
person. It must be remembered also that
this latter group is not composed solely of
single men. Countless families also are
forced to live in unbelievable congestion
in one room, under intolerable conditions
of sanitation and water supply. Under such
circumstances healthy family living, even
in its most humble form, is impossible.

The second point--housing condition--is
more difficult to demonstrate with precise
figures. With Census data it is possible to
determine only that a large share of the
units have walls constructed with non-
permanent materials. But no data are
available to describe the extensive
deterioration in the remaining structures.
Although initially built with pucca [masonry]
materials, many of these buildings permit

conditions of even higher congestion and
offer less light and air to their inhabitants than do kutchha structures.

Important as they are, these existing
problems are overshadowed by the prospect
of the future. Providing adequate
accommodation for the expected increase in
population appears to be an almost insur-
mountable task in itself, let alone the
correction of present ills. To gain some
sense of the magnitude involved an
approximation has been made of the new
housing that would be required to solve
both existing and future needs. This is
based on a few simple standards which
represent a more or less conventional view
of minimum housing.

Table 5 shows that if average standards
of 2.5 persons per room and 2 rooms per
housing unit are used, 430,000 new rooms,
or 215,000 new units, would be needed to
eliminate existing overcrowding and
provide for the houseless population of
1961. Adding the amount required to
accommodate the expected CMD population
growth and maintain the 1961 vacancy
rates, the total 1961-86 requirements would
be 2.5 million new rooms, or 1.3 million
new housing units.[7] If the suggested
space standards were to be met, it would
be necessary to construct new housing units
over these twenty-five years equal to
84 per cent of the total 1961 supply.

These quantities are even more startling
when they are seen in relation to the
current output of the construction industry
in the CMD. It is estimated that in the
early 1960's between 6,000 and 9,000 pucca
units were built per year in the
Metropolitan District. According to
Table 5, however, the accommodation of
new population growth alone requires
53,000 additional units annually.

This of course does not mean that the
population not housed in new pucca
structures is now going homeless. Some
have to accept even further overcrowding

TABLE 5

CMD HOUSING NEEDS ESTIMATE, 1961-86
(in thousands)

	Total Rooms	Total Housing Units	Units/ Year 1961-86
1961 HOUSING STOCK			
Occupied Housing	2,113	1,329	-
Estimated Vacant Housing	95	60	-
Total Housing	2,208	1,389	-
1961-86 REQUIREMENTS[a]			
To eliminate overcrowding and provide for the houseless as of 1961	430	215	11
To accommodate 1961-86[b] growth of non-institutional population	2,112	1,056	53
Provision for Vacancy[c]	114	57	3
Total	2,656	1,328	67

Notes:

a. Assumed Average Standards: a) 2.5 persons per room in
    occupied units; b) 2 rooms per unit average for total
    units. In these estimates, because of the lack of
    adequate base data, no provision is made for one part
    of the total requirement--the replacement of inadequate
    and seriously deteriorated structures.

b. Population: a) 1961 noninstitutional population =
    6,355,000; b) 1961 ratio of noninstitutional population
    to total population = 0.946; c) 1961-86 total population
    growth = 5,580,000; d) 1961-86 noninstitutional
    population growth = 5,279,000.

c. Vacancy Rate: The 1961 rate, 4.32 per cent of total
    housing units, applied to total needs above.

Source: India, Government of West Bengal, Calcutta Metro-
         politan Planning Organisation, Basic Development
         Plan for the Calcutta Metropolitan District, 1966-
         1986 (Calcutta: Public Relations Officer, Calcutta
         Metropolitan Planning Organisation, 1966), p. 28.

in existing housing. A large part of
the remainder have no alternative but
kutchha huts, usually in proliferating
bustee areas, in conditions of filth and
squalor, throughout the CMD. Some must make
do with unused nighttime space in factories,
the passageways of apartment buildings,
alleyways or footpaths.

The results of the present failure to
provide for adequate and sanitary housing,
even at minimum standards, to keep pace with
population expansion are visible throughout
the cities of Calcutta and Howrah, and in
every municipality of the CMD. Everywhere
the picture so far as housing is concerned
is one of deficit and deterioration. It
is characterised by overcrowding, congestion, insanitation, inadequate water
supply, extensive bustee areas, high
rents and premiums. Everywhere there is
a great deal of illegal occupation and
squatting on public and private lands--
whether of refugee colonies built out of
necessity on the vacant lands of absentee
landlords, or of pathetic clusters of
squatters in tattered and improvised
shelters on public pavements, on the
municipal refuse dumps, and indeed on
any vacant site. The urban environment
in Metropolitan Calcutta is probably
deteriorating faster through the sheer
inadequacy of housing, with its attendant
evils, than through any other single cause.

Three basic conclusions seem indisputable.
First, the population estimate of between
12 and 13 million in 1986 may not be further
reduced by planning because that estimate
itself is based on an assumption of the
success of a regional plan for a more
balanced pattern of urbanisation in West
Bengal. Secondly, neither adequate
administrative and fiscal machinery nor
a sufficiently developed construction
industry yet exists in the State to
organise and implement a housing
programme (whether in the public or
private sector) on a scale that even
remotely approaches the indicated housing
need. Thirdly, radical and original

re-thinking of housing standards and of
housing types is necessary to develop
a housing programme on a scale commensurate
with the expected population increase and
at a rate sufficient to curb further
deterioration of the urban environment.[8]

TOWARD A SHELTER PROGRAM BELOW
THE HOUSING THRESHOLD

The remainder of this chapter is devoted to a
discussion of the kinds of shelter programs that
might be initiated below the housing threshold.
There is much more additional work to be done before
implementable solutions can be obtained. This work
will have to be pioneering in nature because nowhere,
to my knowledge, is there a fully effective program
under way, though there are promising starts in
Latin America and India. It is well to recognize
the general inadequacy of trying to transmit Western
concepts and standards to the developing countries.

However, as Hoselitz points out, a great number
of scholars have been expressing views in which they
envisage

. . . that the development of underdeveloped
countries depends not merely upon their
adopting the economic and technological
procedures of the more advanced countries,
but also upon their coming to resemble
them in social structure . . .[9]

This view is supported by Kindleberger and Spengler
in their evaluation of a number of World Bank reports.
Hoselitz's quote from Kindleberger is of particular
interest:

Essentially, however, these are essays in
comparative statics. The missions bring
to the underdeveloped country a notion of
what a developed country is like. They
observe the underdeveloped country.
They subtract the latter from the former.
The difference is a program. Most of
the members of the missions come from
developed countries with highly
articulated institutions for achieving
social, economic, and political ends.

Ethnocentricity leads inevitably to the
conclusion that the way to achieve the
comparable levels of capital formation,
productivity, and consumption is to
duplicate these institutions . . .[10]

It is this "arrogance of technical assistance"
which has so greatly held back the contribution of
the foreign expert in the developing countries.
There is no quick way--no panacea--for the problems
of the developing countries in housing or any other
field. The role of the foreign expert is not to
bring the solutions but to guide the host country
professionals in their search for indigenous
proposals.

One of the reasons for the bad performance of
the developing countries in the housing field has
been the reliance on three apparently reasonable,
but yet unworkable, assumptions which, to a greater
or lesser extent, have been imported from housing
programs of the West. They are: Slums must be
cleared; the housing unit is the basic variable in
the problem; and the government must subsidize the
low-cost housing program because private enterprise
will not play a responsible role.

The first sections of this chapter have tried
to show the futility of these assumptions as the
basis for an approach to the low-cost housing
problem. The evidence is substantial that under
no circumstances can all the slums be cleared and
the people placed in decent sanitary structures. It
becomes obvious, then, that if a solution is to be
found, it must be based on a new set of assumptions,
such as:

The Existing Housing Stock,
Even in Slums, Must Be Preserved

As long as cities in the developing countries
are faced with a rapidly increasing demand for
shelter, coming on top of a very large existing
deficit, it must be recognized that the first
priority must be given to expanding the total
housing supply. This means undertaking slum clearance projects only when there is a clear and
important reuse of the land required. No slum
clearance should be undertaken when the only purpose
is to replace slum housing with standard housing.

Such projects do not add housing units to the total
supply, yet take substantial amounts of public
resources, both financial and administrative, which
could otherwise be used to provide new housing.

The Standard of Living for
Low-Income People Must Be Improved

There is a constant debate about what standards
should be used in building housing for low-income
people. This debate centers on the minimum-housing
unit, and the conclusions reached generally result
in recommended standards so low that it is not
possible to build a really attractive building that
will be an asset in the city, and yet standards far
too high to permit a program at a scale massive
enough to meet the needs. There will never be a
program capable of meeting the housing problem that
is constrained by standards for the housing unit.
Freedom to experiment, to innovate, to get on with
the job is essential. This is not to say that
standards for housing which, in fact, represent
reasonable goals by which to measure the effectiveness of a given housing program should not be
developed. Such standards should only be used,
however, after careful consideration of the means
available for achieving them.

Professor Jakobson develops this point by using
the data on persons per room presented in the U.N.,
Statistical Yearbook, 1963:

> . . . the occupancy rate expressed in
> terms of persons per room is one of the
> few measurable criteria which can be
> easily applied to an assessment of total
> housing demand.

> In economic theory housing programmes
> are often related to some of the general
> indicators of economic progress. Thus,
> for instance, the U.N. expert committee
> on housing related investment in resi-
> dential construction to the total capital
> formation of a country and to its gross
> national product.[11] This prompted an
> investigation to find out whether there
> existed a measurable relationship between
> per capita gross national product and per
> capita housing stock as expressed by the
> room occupancy ratio. Data for some

30 countries in different stages of
economic development and in different
geographic regions were collected and
plotted. The results are shown in
Graph 2. They indicate a reverse
relationship between the two factors
following a curve approximating a
hyperbola.

Although the plotting recorded four
instances of substantial deviation . . .
[which Jakobson explained in his paper],
the record, on the whole, is of
considerable consistency. It is of
interest to note that the upper chord
without exception connects points which
represent countries with severe seasonal
climatic variations resulting in high
construction costs. Countries along
this chord include Sweden and Finland.
Along the lower chord one finds India,
Ceylon, Italy, and Denmark. All of
these have much milder climates.

* * * *

. . . the graph reveals three interesting
benchmarks which can be useful in determining housing goals and standards.
First, one can conclude, that the
"affluent" housing standard of 1 room
per person or more can be obtained only
after the general standard of living has
reached or is about to reach a level
commensurable with a gross national
product of $1,000 (in 1960 prices).
However, occupancy ratios do not improve
significantly after that level has been
reached although the rise in per capita
G.N.P. will continue.

The second bench-mark occurs at a density
of 1.5 person per room which, as previously
mentioned, constitutes the crowding threshold
of the U.S. housing programme. This standard
seems to be obtainable at a per capita
G.N.P. level of approximately $500. The
cluster of nations in the vicinity of
this mark include Chile, Cyprus, Greece,
Japan, Puerto Rico, Poland, Venezuela,
and others.

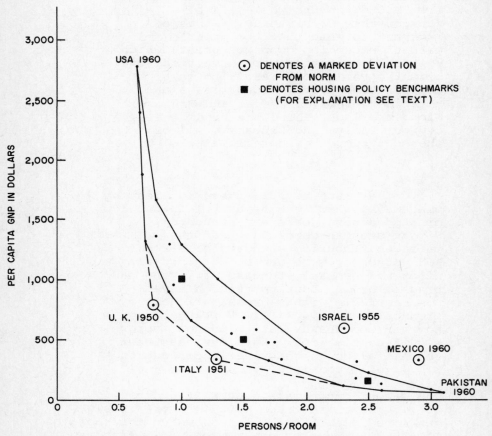

GRAPH 2

OCCUPANCY DENSITY IN RELATION TO PER CAPITA GNP

⊙ DENOTES A MARKED DEVIATION
FROM NORM
■ DENOTES HOUSING POLICY BENCHMARKS
(FOR EXPLANATION SEE TEXT)

USA 1960

U. K. 1950

ITALY 1951

ISRAEL 1955

MEXICO 1960

PAKISTAN 1960

PER CAPITA GNP IN DOLLARS

PERSONS/ROOM

Sources: U. N., Statistical Yearbook, 1963; Barach, The New Europe; Miscellaneous other reports.

The third mark at 2.5 persons per room,
occurs at a G.N.P. level of £150.
Countries in this cluster include Ceylon,
India (on the low side),El Salvador,
Honduras and Yugoslavia.

At this point the question may be asked
how this kind of indicator could be used
as a criterion for the programming of
housing? If one takes, as an example,
the case of India, it is quite obvious
from the graph that a national target
for the next 10-15 years could not
exceed a standard 2.5 persons per
room. . . .[12]

The Total Community Living Environment
Is the Critical Variable,
Not the Housing Unit

The emphasis on most research and experimentation with the problems of low-cost housing has been
with the housing unit. In a country with the warm
climate of India, where living is largely done in
the outside public spaces of the neighborhood, the
stress on the housing unit as a critical variable is
misplaced.

The real problem is not the housing unit, no
matter how humble, but the uncollected human wastes,
the polluted stagnant water which does not drain
away, the inadequate water supply, the dark unlit
lanes, the litter and filth, the nonexistence of
community services, the lack of open space, and the
social and legal problems that come with squatters.

Therefore, the total community is the critical
variable, and the program should be essentially a
total community development program and not just a
series of housing projects.

Private Capital Must Be
Attracted to Low-Cost Shelter

The most crippling of all the attitudes about
low-cost housing is the belief that private capital
has no role to play. This assumption is disproved
by the fact that most of the slums are owned by
private capital, and the new slums being formed at
the edge of the city are being constructed with
private capital. Since it is absolutely certain

that the governments cannot allocate sufficient
funds to housing for low-income people to even
begin to make an effective impact on the problem,
it becomes essential to harness the private capital
already flowing into the low-cost shelter business
to produce a better environment for the tenants,
but at rents they still can afford.

Whatever program is attempted to provide housing
for low-income people, it must be based on a new
approach to government subsidies. Any solution that
calls for 60 per cent subsidy or more by government
is, in fact, no long-range solution at all because
the financing will never be available.

The Test of Any Proposed Solution to the
Low-Cost Shelter Problem Will Be Whether
or Not It Is Capable of Massive
Application to Meet the Needs
of All Low-Income People

There is little value in investing substantial
public resources in any program that benefits only
a small percentage of the low-income people. As has
been shown earlier in this chapter, such a solution
only calls on other low-income people to pay,
through their indirect taxes, for the benefits
given the few people awarded such subsidized housing.
Such an approach is doomed to failure before it
begins, and, in fact, the more housing units that
are built under such programs, the more unfair it
becomes.

The stress must be on devising a total program
that can fully meet the needs of low-income people.
In Calcutta, for instance, it will be necessary to
create a program capable of building 40,000 units a
year on a continuing basis.

Two major and related programs in Calcutta have
been developed to the point where actual work can
now start. Both programs hold the promise of
meeting the assumptions set forth here. The first
of these programs is the Bustee Improvement Program,
designed to make life in the existing bustees less
intolerable. The second is the Low-cost Temporary
Urban Settlement Program, designed to open up vast
new areas for temporary occupancy by low-income
families.

THE BUSTEE IMPROVEMENT PROGRAM

In Calcutta, the word "bustee" is used as a
name for a specific kind of slum development. A
bustee is roughly equivalent to the favella of Brazil,
though there are some differences. "Bustee" is, in
fact, a legal term which describes an area of at
least one sixth of an acre and containing huts. Huts,
under the definition, cannot be built of masonry construction (called "pucca") but must be of temporary
construction using mud, bamboo, straw, and other
loose materials (called "kutchha"). A hut usually
contains eight to ten cubicles, which are rented to
separate families. A bustee also represents a close
set of economic and social relationships. It is, in
the truest sense, a community within the city.

There are 1.2 million people living in bustees
in the Calcutta Metropolitan District, under varying
degrees of squalid living conditions. There are
3,200 separate bustee holdings. The unique character-
istic about the bustee is the three levels of interest.
First, there are the landowners, whose land has been
given over to bustees either by historical events
(some of the bustees in Calcutta are over one hundred
years old) or by squatting. The landowner does not
want the bustee on his land because he can obtain
much higher rents from alternative uses and has
little or no hope of selling his land for anywhere
near the market value of land unencumbered by huts.
There are laws that prohibit the landlord from
clearing the huts. Second, there are the "thika
tenants." There are approximately 20,000 thika
tenants, who own the 30,000 huts. They are supposed
to pay a land rent, but, in fact, collections are
small if paid at all. The thika tenant is frequently
a resident in his own hut. They are small operators
but together form a politically strong association.
Third are the renters, who usually pay about $2.00
per month to live in one room in a hut.

The reasons bustees exist are obvious. They
form the only available pool of shelter that low-
income people can afford. In this sense, the thika
tenant provides an essential service. The bustee is
responsive to the needs of a population and provides
a destination for the in-migrant. An important
consideration in planning for the bustees is that
they generally house a transient and not a stable
population.

The Calcutta Metropolitan Planning Organisation has proposed a major program for the improvement of the bustees. It recognizes that they cannot be cleared in the foreseeable future, but very substantial improvements in the standard of living can be made within the existing bustees at reasonable cost. The following are the physical improvements proposed:

1. A Water System to provide an adequate supply of clean and safe water for the daily needs of bustee residents. It is proposed that tubewells be used to provide water. The typical system would include tubewells; pump houses, with pumping machinery; chlorination; reservoirs; the necessary distribution system and other appurtenances.

2. Community Water Taps and Baths. One water tap for every 100 persons and two baths for every 100 persons are proposed. They will be located in such a way as to be convenient to the residents. The designs are simple, to minimize maintenance. Privacy in the community baths is afforded. It is expected that the bath taps will be used also for water supply, and thus the effective water tap standard will be one water point per 33 persons (or approximately seven families).

3. Sanitary Sewer System. Perhaps the greatest difficulty in most bustees is the lack of sanitary facilities. A sanitary sewer system, including necessary sewers and appurtenances, is proposed.

4. Sanitary Latrines, at a standard of four per 100 people, will provide approximately one sanitary latrine for each hut. Two or four latrines will be placed in appropriate structures so located that maximum accessibility will be afforded. All service privies will be demolished.

5.   Storm Drainage System. Inadequate or
      nonexistent storm drainage facilities
      presently result in washouts of structures,
      flooding, and generally unsafe and insani-
      tary conditions, especially during the
      monsoon periods. These deficiencies
      will be corrected by the proposed storm
      drainage system, which will include
      necessary inlets.

6.   Pavements will supplement the storm
      drainage system and provide safe and
      clean paths where they do not
      presently exist.

7.   Lighting in the crowded bustees is
      essential for the safety and convenience
      of the residents. Street lighting is
      proposed at regular intervals and at
      crucial locations where walkways
      cross or turn.

8.   Treatment of Tanks. Tanks are found
      in almost all bustees and at present
      constitute health hazards in nearly
      all cases. It is proposed that they
      be treated in a variety of ways, the
      method selected depending upon the
      conditions prevailing in individual
      bustees.

      Wherever possible, tanks will be
      preserved and made sanitary to elimi-
      nate whatever health hazards remain,
      after sewerage has been provided and
      service privies have been removed.
      They will also be improved by planting
      and other means to refresh and enliven
      the physical environment and add to
      their attractiveness as centres of
      community activity. In bustees in
      which additional land is needed
      urgently for community facilities
      tanks will be cleansed and improved
      over part of their area and the remaining
      area will be filled to provide the
      necessary space. These two alternative
      methods are the ones to be preferred,
      since they preserve the usefulness of
      the tanks for bathing, retain them as
      cool retreats against the summer heat,

and enhance their aesthetic value.
As a third alternative, where it is
essential for health purposes or to
provide additional buildable space,
tanks will be completely filled.[13]

A basic part of the concept is that the landowners' interests will be purchased, by a combination
of bonds and cash, so that the land will become an
urban land bank for the future development of the
city. As clearance of bustees becomes financially
possible or when important new uses must be sited
within the city, land will be available, and the
profits from the reuse of the land will accrue to
the public.

It is not proposed to disturb the rights of the
thika tenants who will then pay ground rents to the
government. The basis of the compensation has been
proposed at thirty times the annual rent received
by the landlords. It is not expected that the landlords will object as this capital invested elsewhere
will greatly improve their returns.

The program also calls for the vigorous undertaking of an urban community development program.
Both the Public Land Acquisition Program and the
Urban Community Development Program are basic parts
of the second major program to create new temporary
urban settlements on the edges of the city.

THE LOW-COST TEMPORARY
URBAN SETTLEMENT PROGRAM

If uncontrolled slum formation is to be
prevented in the future, it will be necessary to
devise a program to provide mass housing. Such a
program cannot look to large government subsidies
to meet its requirements but must rely on the people
themselves to pay for their own shelter. This means
that housing of the cost now being built by low-
income people must form the essential ingredient in
any mass housing program. The funds available from
government should be allocated to providing an urban
environment, whereby the most detrimental effects
of this type of housing can be minimized and the
in-migrants introduced to urban living. Such a
program calls for the acquisition of large land
areas to provide project sites and the installation
of the community facilities necessary for a decent
and healthy life.

Calcutta's proposed Low-cost Temporary Urban Settlement Program is a logical extension of the Bustee Improvement Program scheduled for the existing slum areas. The same kinds of improvements will be provided at the same standards. In addition, there would be an over-all development plan for each area which would lay out the communities in an organized way. Community facilities, such as schools, dispensaries, and play space, would also be intro- duced--but using temporary buildings.

These areas would then be equal to the improved bustees, with better community facilities, and far superior to the slum accommodations otherwise available at the same general rent. If sufficient improved land is made available to absorb the full growth of the population, then it should be possible to use the police power to prevent squatting and uncontrolled bustee formation on the edges of the city.

The idea that these areas will be temporary is an essential part of the over-all concept. It is often said that there is nothing so permanent as temporary housing. And the difficulties of moving people-- particularly low-income people--from their homes are well known. The concept of "temporary" as used in this program is somewhat different from other proposals for temporary housing units in that it assumes occupancy up to fifteen years. All structures to be built will be restricted to one-story buildings. The financing of the structures will be so arranged that the units are completely amortized by the end of the time period when it is proposed to terminate the housing in a particular location. This program is based on the assumption of an on-going development program building upwards of 40,000 units per year. This will insure a constant supply of relocation housing always within a short distance of the existing housing, which is to be eliminated for other higher economic uses.

Basic to the concept, and underlying the need for housing of this type to be temporary, is the assumption of continuous growth of the city. The sites selected for temporary housing areas will be on lands at the fringe of the city, which in ten or fifteen years will be required for permanent con- struction of industry or other types of housing. The necessary roads and utilities can be put in in advance and used for the temporary housing on the site and then converted to the permanent uses

later on. The residents of the temporary housing
can be relocated to a similar facility a short
distance away. In this manner, the city can expand
in a logical and economical pattern--the urban land
required for permanent construction coming into the
market in a systematic and organized process in the
locations required by the over-all development plan.

If temporary occupancy of land on the urban
fringe by low-cost housing, followed by the use of
the land for permanent urban construction, can be
made to work, many very significant problems of city
growth dynamics can be solved. At the moment, the
fringe of the city is rapidly proliferating into a
new ring of slums that threaten to choke the city's
future growth. In the absence of enforceable police
powers and in the face of the overwhelming need for
shelter space, the city stands powerless to control
this growth. All techniques of trying to establish
low-income housing projects at great distances from
the city center and places of employment have always
failed, yet it is only in outlying areas that land
costs are low enough to permit such projects. By
introducing the idea of a temporary use of urban
fringe land, both problems are solved. The development, which is going on regardless, becomes controlled,
and the location is close enough to be attractive.

An additional benefit of the concept of low-cost
temporary housing is the opportunity of building at
higher standards later on. The great shortage of
funds and the pressures of the problem have combined
to produce so-called minimum standards for permanent
housing that are so low that they may well produce
future slums. Housing built today with a life
expectancy of at least sixty years sets the form of
the future city in brick and concrete. It is not
unreasonable to expect--and as a minimum hope--that
the Indian city of the twenty-first century can be
a vastly better place to live: Birth control can
become effective; alternative places of rural-to-
urban migration developed; the national economy
greatly strengthened; and new construction technology
become available. To postpone as much as possible
the commitment of large areas of urban space to forms
of development that may prove totally unsatisfactory
in the future seems logical and appropriate at this
stage of India's development.

The land acquired under such a program would
form an urban land bank of great value in assisting

the eventual renewal of the city in the years ahead.
The best that can be done today may be unacceptable
in the future, but if temporary housing communities
are built and the land brought under public control,
the renewability of the city is assured, and eventual
permanent construction can be in tune with the
conditions of the future.

The obvious difficulty with this approach to
temporary housing and the organized expansion of the
city is the demonstrated reluctance of the government
to take the necessary actions required to relocate
families. This problem, in the end, must be faced
if progress of any sort is to be made in the city.
Development progress throughout history has never
been painless. The less money available, the more
painful the transition of development has been for
the people. There is no substitute for the rigorous
prosecution of the development program. No plan, no
matter how promising, will ever implement itself.
The final test of progress will be whether or not
the hard decisions are made that will permit an
aggressive management of the program. In this
respect, these proposals for a low-cost temporary
settlement program are no different from any other
proposals made for the development of Calcutta.

In order to undertake a massive urban settlement
program, it is necessary to identify the individual
components of which it will consist. They can be
divided into two groups: those costs that must be
amortized with the useful life of the housing unit
and those costs that are convertible into assets at
the end of the useful life of the housing unit.

If the proposed settlement program is to be
without direct subsidy, it is necessary to assign
each of these costs to a source of revenue sufficient
to meet the cost. The tenant is the obvious source
of revenue, and in the private housing market, he
carries the project without subsidy and yields a
profit to the housing promoter and investors.
However, to meet the massive housing needs of the
lowest-income people, the monthly rents must not
exceed $2.00 per month, and rentals at that level
are not sufficient to cover the total cost.

The most likely way to reduce the total cost to
the tenant is to free the tenant from the cost of
the land and the carrying charges. This can be done
either by subsidy, which has been rejected here as

precluding a truly massive program, or by passing on
the cost of the land to other parties. This latter
possibility deserves full exploration.

In the rising land-price situation found in the
Calcutta area today, it is reasonable to suppose that
the value of the land will increase during the life-
time of the project. This increase in value, if it
maintains a rate of increase equal to the cumulative
interest rate on the capital invested in the land,
can be realized upon the sale of the land at the
end of the project period to its ultimate public or
private user. The lender of the original capital is
then paid off in a lump sum with accumulated interest.

The obvious source of funds for this type of
investment would be the government. These loans,
which are in many ways very similar to those made
internationally between developed and developing
countries, would be a much better investment than
the present system of subsidizing housing directly.
At the end of ten or fifteen years, depending on
the project's planned life, the government would
have its capital returned in full, with interest,
as opposed to losing between 60-70 per cent in the
form of subsidy in a permanent pucca housing project.

There are many other planning advantages as
well. The government could sell the land for private
construction according to the over-all development
plan for an area, thereby controlling the ultimate
construction of the site. An urban land bank will
be created, which will make available sites for
public purpose projects at optimum locations.
Because land assembly will have been done, the
ultimate private development of the site will be
more efficient, thereby reducing the cost of public
services and simplifying the process of development
by the private purchaser.

The cost of improvements of the site, such as
land filling, main roads, trunk sewers, and water
mains, can also be charged to the ultimate developer.
Since these facilities have useful lives of fifty
to one hundred years, they will be represented by
the increase in the value of the land.

The costs of the project that are tied to the
life of the housing units must be carried by the
tenant. The largest of these is the cost of the
unit itself. Obviously, permanent construction

of the type now being developed by government in the
slum clearance program is too expensive, even if the
land costs are not carried by the tenant. Such high
building costs are not necessary in the type of
temporary housing scheme under consideration here.
Immediate savings can be made by placing the water
taps, baths, and latrines outside the dwelling unit
on a shared basis. Further savings can be made by
building only one-story buildings not requiring
piling, structural steel, thick walls, and interior
public spaces, such as stairwells. Instead of square-
foot construction costs near $3.50, there should be
no difficulty in providing semi-pucca shell housing
under $.40 per square foot, amortized over a
fifteen-year project life.

The problem of rent collection and management
is found in all housing projects run by the government.
There is a great reluctance on the part of government
to enforce rent collection procedures, and the powers
of eviction are difficult to use effectively. Rent
collection frequently does not even cover the cost
of management, let alone make a contribution toward
paying for the project itself.

It is proposed that the thika tenant system,
partially modified, be continued in the Low-cost
Temporary Urban Settlement Program. To do so, will
result in many substantial advantages to the program.
Among them are:

a) The thika tenant becomes a buffer between
the occupants of the housing and the government.
Since the government is only the landlord and not
the hut owner, no protests over standards of the
housing, treatment of the occupants, or methods of
operation can be mounted effectively against the
government.

b) Since the thika tenant will be responsible
for collecting rents, selecting tenants, and, if
necessary, evicting, the government's responsibility
for management is greatly reduced, and its source
of income from the project will be more reliable.

c) The thika tenant will bring to the project
the necessary private capital for the individual
shelter units, thereby substantially reducing the
over-all cost to government for the project. The
methods used to attract the private capital can be
flexible to permit thika tenants to own various
numbers of shelter units.

d) The thika tenant system provides income and employment to individuals who might otherwise take a job that could be filled by someone else.

The government would enter into a lease agreement with each thika tenant regarding the time of occupancy of the site, the land rent to be paid, the services and facilities the government would provide, and the standards required for the individual shelter units. Government might also consider building the shelter units directly and selling them to the individual thika tenants.

If the Low-cost Temporary Urban Settlement Program is implemented at the scale proposed here, the supply of shelter units should be great enough that rents will be kept reasonable by the law of supply and demand.

THE URBAN COMMUNITY DEVELOPMENT PROGRAM

It is not enough to merely make improvements in the physical environment available to the slum dweller. There is a need to assist him in the social transition required for urban living. Basic to the Bustee Improvement Program and the Low-cost Temporary Urban Settlement Program is the initiation of an Urban Community Development Program.

The objectives of this supporting program can be summarized as follows:

a) to secure the willing consent, cooperation, and participation of the bustee dwellers themselves, to the maximum extent possible, in the implementation of the program of the bustee improvement.

b) to achieve, through the individual response and collective responsibility of the bustee dwellers, the most effective use and maintenance of the physical improvements installed.

c) to supplement physical improvement with an intensive program of health education (including a campaign for mass immunization).

d) to organize and encourage, through voluntary leadership, a concerted effort toward community welfare and development within the improved bustees.

In all the existing bustee areas, there are a
wide variety of clubs and organizations representing
every facet of community life. To be successful, a
government-sponsored program should not seek to
impose a new form of activity but, rather, should
seek to harness and use more effectively that which
now exists. In this sense, the Urban Community
Development Program will bring together into an
integrated team the voluntary organizations on the
one hand and the government service agencies, such
as clinics and birth control centers, on the other.

THE SOCIAL IMPLICATIONS

There is a substantial body of literature that
has been developed over the years on the general
subject of "Who are the slum dwellers?" Yet, the
results of these studies have not been successfully
translated into the design of housing projects.
The present slum clearance projects have been
severely criticized for their lack of adaptability
of the real needs of the slum dweller. The Low-cost
Temporary Urban Settlement Program offers an
opportunity to correct some of these failings.

The type of shelter proposed here represents
a general continuation of the traditional forms of
housing to which lowest-income people are accustomed.

The bustee hut with its confined physical space
defines one level of social space in the slum area--
it sets the pattern of neighboring. Even in cases
where there are distinct religious differences, the
proximity of living areas seems to stimulate integration. This close proximity is not possible in the
design of the four-story walk-up structures built
for slum clearance housing.

The one-story structure is also generally
preferred by slum dwellers. It represents the
traditional and familiar form of housing and has
the practical advantage of immediate access to the
open areas where so much of the slum dweller's time
is spent in both work and leisure.

The fact that the structures proposed for the
Low-cost Temporary Urban Settlement Program will
be only partially finished, and, therefore, provide
a very flexible arrangement for interior space, is
another substantial advantage over the pucca slum

clearance housing projects. Slum dwellers, because
of their low incomes and marginal standard of living,
need to make the maximum use of their living space.
Permanent flats allow no adjustment to the very wide
range of family sizes and incomes of the slum
dwellers, but the proposed temporary shelters would
have complete flexibility. It would permit the
development of workshops, home industries, schools,
and sanitary animal shelters within the project areas.
It would permit a family to acquire as much space
as his family requires and his income can permit.
This flexibility is possible because of the nature
of the structure to be provided and the basic fact
that the management of the shelter will be in
private hands, thereby minimizing the number of rules
and regulations that accompany government projects.

Government will still have a major administrative
task in selecting thika tenants and assigning appropriate shelter units to them. The four main social
factors to be considered are: language, place of
origin, vocation, and religion. The natural process
at work in the bustees promotes social integration
and harmony in the various slum areas by recognizing
these important factors in their development process.
So, too, in the new low-cost housing areas these
factors must be considered in making assignments to
thika tenants representing the various communities
that must be served and making the provision of
community facilities, such as schools (in the
mother tongue), libraries, and social clubs as
convenient as possible.

The process whereby a particular low-cost
temporary urban settlement becomes developed and
occupied requires careful planning. At present,
the new migrant to the city comes alone and leaves
his family in the village until he is settled. He
goes to friends, usually from the same village, in
a particular bustee and stays with them. It is
unlikely that these migrants can be attracted to
the low-cost urban settlement areas directly. The
very long-term bustee residents who have lived more
than twenty years in a particular bustee are also
very reluctant to move to any new location. In the
beginning, therefore, the people most likely to be
attracted to the new areas are the residents of the
bustees who have been here from one to ten years
and are somewhat settled but still have not
established permanent attachments to the bustee
where they are located.

THE HOUSING THRESHOLD   101

In the beginning, it will be necessary to attract
people to the new areas by extensive publicity and by
taking groups of potential thika tenants out to the
sites to see the areas for themselves. An organized
effort to do this will be necessary on the part of the
government organization responsible for the project.
Once the social character of a particular settlement
area is established, it will tend to be self-
perpetuating, as new migrants will then come to stay
with the residents already in the project area. Once
again, the flexibility of the physical plan of the
low-cost temporary urban settlements makes accommodation of these future residents much easier than would
be the case with pucca structures.

These many very important social considerations
are compatible with the Low-cost Temporary Urban
Settlement Program proposed here. They add up to
an additional important argument for this type of
solution to the shelter problems of lowest-income
people.

The general conclusions drawn from the work in
Calcutta are indirectly supported in the work under
way in Madras and Delhi. These cities are already
undertaking variations of low-cost temporary urban
settlements, with various degrees of success. Most
interesting is that officials in both cities do not
point with any particular pride to these projects,
even though they seem to be reasonably popular with
the people who are living in them. There are
various reasons for this, but the most apparent is
the belief that, somehow, government should be
providing better housing and not creating new slums,
no matter how much better the standard of living in
them may be. Nonetheless, it is useful to review
these projects to assess the strengths and weaknesses
of this approach to low-cost housing.

THE MADRAS EXPERIENCE

The Madras State Housing Board has earned the
distinction of being one of the best house-building
organizations in India. Since the formation of the
Board in 1961 (out of the old Madras Improvement
Trust) until today, Madras has been fortunate in
having a highly motivated and active housing program.
Under the dynamic leadership of the senior officers,
Madras has consistently sought out, and spent, more
than its allotted share of central government

subsidies by absorbing the unused quotas of other
states. Furthermore, the Housing Board has enjoyed
the confidence of the state government and has
received state funds beyond the immediate obligations
imposed by the central schemes. In short, Madras
has a proud and impressive record of success in the
house-building field. Under existing conditions,
it is difficult to see how they could have done any
better.

Up to 1966, the Madras State Housing Board had
built 10,372 dwelling units and developed 7,451
plots. Of these, 4,658 units and 6,658 open-land
plots were for relocation of slum families.

The significant fact, acknowledged by everyone
in Madras, is that there are vastly more people
living in slums today than in 1950. In 1950, it was
estimated that there were approximately three hundred
slum areas. Since then, one hundred eighty areas
have been cleared--a sizable achievement by any
criteria--yet, today they estimate that about seven
hundred slum areas exist. Roughly six lakhs (a lakh
equals 100,000) of people live in these slum
areas--more than double the 1950 slum population.
These figures stand in grim evidence to the futility
of existing slum clearance techniques. It can be
concluded that if Madras--with its expertise and a
comparatively well-financed program--cannot dent the
slum problem, then no major Indian city can.

The Madras State Housing Board has experimented
with two types of low-cost housing: open-plot
development and transit housing camps. The latter
consist of large buildings of about eight units
each made of country wood frames covered with woven
coconut matting and low brick walls. These units
are used to house families from the slum areas during
the time that the permanent tenements are being built
on the original site. The usual duration of a family's
stay in the transit housing is about one year, then
they move to their tenement unit, often back on the
very site they occupied as squatters. Because the
transit camps are considered short-term housing, no
environmental facilities have been provided on a
permanent basis. The latrines are of concrete
construction. The water supply is carried in from
tubewells and taps located on nearby streets. The
paths are not paved, and there is no lighting.
As a result, the transient camps provide a very low
standard of housing, really no better than that found

in the slum areas themselves. There is no rent
charged in the transient camp. About six hundred
units of this type of housing are provided. The
reason for not improving the site to a level of the
environmental standards used in the open plot areas
is the desire of the State Housing Board to make it
absolutely clear that the transient camps are only
temporary locations for short-term occupancy.

Open-plot development, on the other hand, is
considered permanent housing. They provide 1,000
square feet per family, but at an over-all density
of twenty-five units per acre, with a 20-by-30 mud
platform, a concrete lavatory and bath (Rs. 650-
Rs. 750) in one corner of the plot, so that one
lavatory and bath unit containing four lavatory-bath
pairs can be placed at the corner of four lots and
serve four families. In addition, each family
receives Rs. 250 worth of raw materials in the form
of bamboo, thatch, etc., and Rs. 32.50 each, the
latter to be used for the employment of skilled
labor, which is combined with the labor of the tenant
himself in the construction of the unit. Thus, the
total construction cost, excluding the cost of the
land, is approximately Rs. 1,000 per family. For
these units, the families are charged Rs. 3 per
month; however, only about half the rents are
actually collected.

These open-plot units were constructed on the
basis of combined state and central financing, with
a very high level of subsidy involved because of
land costs and facilities. The state does not want
to raise the rent to a level that would pay for the
projects. As most of the open-plot schemes are
located on the periphery of the city, and to induce
people to take up residence there, the rents must be
very low to compensate for transport inconvenience
involved. Also, one alternative to living in the
open-plot units is to squat on open land and pay no
rent at all. The open-plot units are not sold on a
hire-purchase basis for it is felt that this would
lead to resale of the plots to persons for whom the
plots were not intended. The open-plot developments
were built as part of a large scheme that included
approximately 1,000 open plots and 1,000 tenements.

All tenements constructed by the State of Madras
are maintained by the state, but the open-plot
schemes are not maintained by the state. It is
up to the rentee to repair his hut, bath, or flush

latrine if they fall into disrepair. The open-plot
schemes are, however, managed totally by the state;
that is, all rent collection is done by the State
Housing Board, and the property is all retained by
the state. The State Housing Board does not have
any social management program to introduce residents
to the correct operation of the facilities.

The open-plot developments seem to be popular
with the residents. They feel that they have more
space than in the tenements, the rents are lower
(tenements rent for Rs. 10 per month), and they
prefer the feeling that the structure is their own.
The State Housing Board, on the other hand, feels
that open-plot development, for them, is very
expensive in the sense that it is heavily subsidized
and rent collection is disappointing. Furthermore,
there is a reluctance on the part of Board officials
to accept this type of housing as being a satisfactory
solution to housing lowest-income people. Nonetheless,
there are plans for developing another 5,000 units.

THE JHUGGI JHONPRI SCHEME, NEW DELHI

Many of the ideas for low-cost housing have been
tried in various forms in India. One of the better
known of these attempts is the Jhuggi Jhonpri Scheme
in New Delhi. Here, approximately 20,000 families
have been moved to resettlement sites at the rate of
about 2,000 families per month. Though the sponsors
of the project within the Municipal Corporation of
Delhi do not think the program has made any appreciable
reduction in the number of squatters and other slum
families in the city, it still represents a sizable
program effort.

The program is thought of as a relocation
scheme. Agencies requiring sites occupied by
squatters request the Delhi Housing Commission to
remove the families to a site within the Jhuggi
Jhonpri Scheme. When the decision is made to move
on a particular site, municipal corporation trucks,
along with demolition gangs and police, execute the
move quickly, taking each family, along with its
possessions and the building materials of their
present hut, to the new site. Here, they are
usually allocated a 25-square-yard plot. (There
are also 80-square-yard plots and apartment blocks
used in the Scheme, but their relevance to the
low-cost housing recommendations in this chapter is
less significant.) The family then erects their
own shelter on the plot assigned.

The family is given a one-year lease by means of a site allocation slip. The rent of the site is generally around Rs. 6 a month, but, in fact, rent collection is so haphazard and difficult that monies realized in this way fail to even cover the cost of administration. Frequently, the tenant will elect to sell the rights to a site to another party not otherwise eligible for prices ranging between Rs. 100-Rs. 200. This practice is particularly true in areas with the 80-square-yard sites. The family then moves back into slums of the city. As a result, some parties have been able to obtain "allocation slips" to two or three contiguous plots and erect substantial pucca houses. The general opinion seems to be that nothing can be done about these houses once constructed--albeit illegally.

The housing that is constructed on the 25-square-yard plots is primarily of a mud brick nature; however, some concrete and brick structures have also been built. Site coverage is up to 75 per cent. Community facilities are on a shared basis: one latrine per five families and one bath per six families. These facilities are located in pucca structures at the end of the rows of plots. Water is supplied through tubewells. The over-all plot layout is of a general superblock concept, with a gridiron system of pedestrian pathways about ten feet in width. Most of the housing has three common walls with its neighbors. The average cost per unit is Rs. 1,000.

A large number of commercial and semi-industrial uses are carried on within the project sites. The plan itself allocates space for commercial activities, but nothing has been done formally to utilize these areas. As a result, many small commercial enterprises, mostly selling tea, pan (a betel leaf preparation), and other minor goods, have sprung up as squatters on the fringe of the project and along the major roads. Many of the project families are conducting some kind of semi-industrial activity on their plot sites as well. Handicraft industries, the reprocessing of scrap metal, cutting of scrap wood into kindling, and other such activities are extensive.

There is a site management office at each area, and these offices have an authorized strength of over ten persons each. In practice, there are many vacancies on the management staffs, and the over-all management of the projects is very lax. There is no programed effort to tie social services or urban community development activities into the program.

Many people consider the Jhuggi Jhonpri Scheme
to be an inadequate solution to the slum problem.
It has many critics and detractors that consider it
a failure. Though there is much that can be improved,
there is no doubt that it is an important step in the
right direction. Basically, it has proved conclus-
ively that this type of housing can be provided on
a massive scale if land is available. It has proved
that the slum inhabitants will accept this type of
housing (though the very distant sites selected have
caused much hardship, and this is the reason given
by those families that have left to return to the
city slums).

Its shortcomings are glaring, but correctable.
A better land-use plan is a matter of design. The
lack of management can be overcome by trying
alternative management proposals. The distance to
the city and places of employment can be overcome
through the concept of temporary housing sites and
the movement of the low-cost housing site always to
the immediate fringe of the city, but always where
it can be connected with good mass-transit facilities.

In short, the Jhuggi Jhonpri Scheme provides
clear proof of the underlying value of the concept
of low-cost housing as a mass solution to improving
the living environment of lowest-income people and
should prove to be the cornerstone for still better
projects that are possible at even less direct cost
to government.

The low-cost housing experience in both Madras
and Delhi points to similar conclusions. Most
surprisingly, and this is supported by the experience in Calcutta as well, the slum dweller does not
seem to be highly motivated to desire high-quality
housing. There is no sense of critical importance
placed on housing. In fact, it is apparent that the
location of living space is more important than
quality of living space. When pressed for information on what kind of housing they wanted, their
comments almost invariable turned on points in the
environment--particularly better water supply and
drainage.

This conclusion was also drawn by John Turner
in several studies done in Latin America. The current
emphasis placed on providing, at largely public
expense, "standard" housing units for lowest-income
people may be an allocation of resources not in

accordance with the priorities that they would choose
for themselves. Low-cost housing of the kinds found
in Madras and Delhi schemes may reflect the aspirations of the lowest-income people more accurately
than the vastly more expensive tenement housing
also provided.

It is obvious, however, that both the Madras
and Delhi schemes fall far short of the optimum
level that is possible in this type of housing.
Management of the projects has proved to be extremely
difficult in both cities, and the low level of rent
collection is a clear indication of the difficulty.
There is a phenomenon which is frequently alluded
to by officials: The lowest-income people, once
admitted to public housing, seem to feel that because
it is government housing they should not be required
to pay rent. This, of course, makes an impossible
management situation, which must be corrected if
there is to be a successful housing program for
lowest-income people.

CONCLUSION

India has made great progress in changing the
concept of housing from sterile public housing for
the few to environmental improvement programs for
the many. The Calcutta program and the efforts in
Madras and New Delhi will, hopefully, become the
pattern for the future. Similar efforts are under
way in Latin America, and more and more literature
in support of this approach is appearing. Among
professionals in the field, the futility of past
housing efforts for lowest-income people is well
known and documented. The future is still uncertain,
but new concepts and approaches are under active
experimentation. It is likely that from these
efforts the solution to this--the most perplexing
of problems--will eventually emerge.

NOTES TO CHAPTER 4

1.   Leland S. Burns, Housing as Social Overhead Capital, Essays in Urban Land Economics (Los Angeles: University of California, 1966), p. 13.

2.   Charles Abrams, Man's Struggle for Shelter in an Urbanizing World (Cambridge: The M.I.T. Press, 1964), p. 54.

3.   Journal of the Institute of Town Planners (India), No. 3 (July, 1955), p. 1.

4.   Rs. 1,000 equals $140.

5.   One crore of rupees is equal to $1.4 million.

6.   Stanislaw H. Wellisz, "India's Slum Clearance Policy: An Economic Evaluation" (unpublished paper, Calcutta Metropolitan Planning Organisation, January, 1967).

7.   This amount, as vast as it is, would not create a totally "satisfactory" housing supply by 1986, since it leaves out any provision for the replacement of structures in substandard condition. At present there is no reliable estimate of replacement needs.

8.   India, Government of West Bengal, Calcutta Metropolitan Planning Organisation, Basic Development Plan for the Calcutta Metropolitan District, 1966-1986 (Calcutta: Public Relations Officer, Calcutta Metropolitan Planning Organisation, 1966), pp. 27-29.

9.   Bert F. Hoselitz, Sociological Aspects of Economic Growth (Chicago: 1960), p. 55.

10.   C. P. Kindleberger, "Review of the Economy of Turkey; the Economic Development of Guatemala; Report on Cuba," Review of Economics and Statistics, Vol. 34, No. 4 (November, 1952), as quoted in Hoselitz, op. cit., p. 55; Measures for the Economic Development of Underdeveloped Countries (New York: United Nations, 1957); Joseph J. Spengler, "IBRD Mission Economic Growth Theory," American Economic Review, Vol. 44, No. 2 (May, 1954).

11. United Nations, Department of Economic and Social Affairs, <u>Report of the Ad Hoc Group of Experts on Housing and Urban Development</u> (New York: United Nations, 1962), p. 1.

12. Leo Jakobson, "Housing Deficiency and Housing Goals and Standards: Criteria for Measurement and Policy" (unpublished paper, Calcutta Metropolitan Planning Organisation, January, 1967), pp. 54-55.

13. India, Government of West Bengal, Calcutta Metropolitan Planning Organisation, <u>op. cit.</u>, pp. 92-93.

CHAPTER **5** PLANNING EDUCATION
FOR DEVELOPMENT

William L. C. Wheaton*

THE MIGRANT TRAINEE

During the past twenty years, Western educational
institutions have launched hundreds, if not thousands,
of educational programs intended to train people for
the developing countries. Some of these are directed
toward natives of those countries, others toward
Westerners who intend to work in the developing
countries. Still others have no distinguishing
features directed toward the problems of developing
areas, but merely provide aid for foreign students
in the conventional professional or scientific
programs of Western institutions.

This chapter is concerned specifically with the
problems of training native personnel to engage in
the planning activities involved in economic growth,
urbanization, and modernization. In so limiting the
topic, I am excluding educational opportunities for
individuals who desire a Western education, who
desire to migrate to more developed countries, or
who are concerned with securing a professional
education not specifically directed toward the
problems of development. This is a very broad
exclusion, for it may eliminate from consideration
a very large proportion of the students now coming
to Western countries for higher education.

---

*William L. C. Wheaton, A.B., Ph.D., is a
Member of the Board of Directors of PADCO, Inc.,
and Dean of the College of Environmental Design,
University of California, Berkeley.

I make this exclusion because it is evident
that most students coming to the United States for
professional and graduate education have very mixed
motives. Apparently, many have no desire to return
to their native countries or, if they have that
desire, they lose it in the ensuing years. A recent
survey of engineering graduates at the University of
California indicates that 50 per cent of those who
received a Bachelor of Engineering degree during the
decade 1950-60 were not practicing in their native
countries at the time of the survey in 1965. Of
those receiving a Masters in Engineering, 30 per cent
never returned to their native countries for professional practice, and of those receiving a Ph.D.,
60 per cent never returned.[1] This is, to be sure,
a limited sample, but in a profession where
experience may be quite analogous to that of
planners, architects, and other professions. At
one time, virtually all of our Fulbrights from
abroad sought permission to stay in the United States.

These figures are wholly understandable. After
all, the students who get to the Western educational
institutions are probably of very superior caliber.
They are probably among the best in their native
countries, encouraged by their professors to complete
their education in the West. Presumably, also, the
fact that they are far from home demonstrates that
they are more ambitious as well as more talented
than their other colleagues who never made the
effort or who did not succeed. After such superior
students have had two or three years in the United
States or some other Western country, they are quite
competitive in talent with the natives of that
country, and they will naturally receive job offers
reasonably comparable to those available to their
fellow graduate students. Given the opportunity to
live in the far richer environment of the West, it
is wholly understandable that many of them should
elect to stay there.

Further, we all know that the opportunities for
professional practice in the West are often more
advantageous than opportunities in the developing
countries. The level of professional equipment and
facilities is better than that available in the
developing countries. The opportunities to pursue
specialized personal interests are typically far
greater. Indeed, much of professional education
that is directed toward the strengthening of
professional values may serve to reinforce the

students' desire to stay in the West, where those
values can be realized more fully, rather than to
undertake the social challenges that so often must
be pursued under less advantageous professional
circumstances.

I fully appreciate that these conditions will
vary widely from country to country and will be
influenced by an enormous range of circumstances.
In some professions and countries, private practice
is common; in others, public practice is almost
universal. In some countries, government service
is handicapped by incredible conditions of bureau-
cratization, which impair or absolutely prevent the
full utilization of young, ambitious professional
talents. In other countries, government agencies
may be responding quickly to great social and
professional challenge. In some countries, the
influence of the professions on policy behavior is
high; in other countries, it is at a low ebb.
In some, the standard of living for the professional
is superior to that in the West; in others, it is
vastly lower. In some, the rate of development is
rapid; in others, it is negative or nonexistent.
Nationalist fervor, coupled with confidence in the
future, may encourage students to return. The
absence of these may deter the acceptance of the
social or national responsibilities for which
students have been prepared. Under these circumstances, any generalization is subject to many
qualifications. Nevertheless, I contend that
graduate and professional students have a high
propensity to stay in the developed countries and
that this must be a primary fact in shaping the
strategy to improve planning personnel for these
countries. I do not argue that we should deprive
individuals of the opportunity for advancement or
migration. I merely contend that we should
recognize the limited value of certain programs for
the purposes of aiding the developing countries.

Even if these premises are accepted and if we
recognize that conventional types of professional
education are relatively inefficient means for
helping developing countries, it may still be
necessary for us to continue programs that involve
attrition rates of 50-80 per cent because we
cannot devise other means. The purpose of this
chapter is to explore some of these alternatives.

THE SCOPE OF THE PLANNING REQUIRED

Before proceeding, I should also define the scope of planning under consideration. While I include persons trained in city or regional planning as it has been taught in the United States or England and which is concerned primarily with the planning of physical development, the needs of the developing countries are far broader. They require experts in public administration, economics and finance, sociology, engineering, architecture, law, public health, and other professional or scientific disciplines. Development must also embrace both physical growth and the expansion of social services that accompany urbanization. For these reasons, we must be concerned with a rather broad spectrum of professions, and we must draw heavily upon the social sciences. People trained in all of these disciplines will find a place in development in national and local government; in ministries concerned with planning and transportation, housing, industrial growth, and agricultural development; in private business; in educational institutions; in cooperative societies; and in independent, civic, research, and other types of organizations. In many countries, the most urgent needs, indeed, may be outside of the main operating agencies of government that appear to have responsibility for development. Unless our thinking is concerned with the whole process of modernization, we will fall short of any reasonably conceived set of objectives.

A part of the strategy of education for development should include an identification of the fields that will have high leverage. In India, one might concentrate heavily upon professions in the civil service. In Chile, the training of private savings and loan society managers might have had a higher payoff. Obviously, such educational planning must rely upon estimates of the sectors of the economy that have the greatest potential for growth at different future periods.

EXISTING RESOURCES

The recruitment of students can also be a vital part of the process. Our present selection procedures are almost random, since the receiving institutions have little contact with the

undergraduate institutions of applicants.
Presumably, the best recruits are those who have
already entered service in development, who can
benefit most from further training, and who will
most surely return to the field. I would, therefore,
give first priority to on-the-job training systems,
short courses in the field and other in-service types
of effort, followed by refresher courses of short
duration.

Since our objective is to expand quantity,
however, we must reach beyond those already
recruited. Here we must note that some countries
have excellent undergraduate programs, including
professional programs. These schools, with graduates
of excellent skills, are clearly the best source of
people who will need only supplementary work on
planning and development problems and procedures.
These students have the additional advantage of a
professional skill and status, to which planning
skills can be added.

In other countries, however, there may be no
educational institutions, or a very thin base.
The United Nations has experimented with a
subprofessional program in Ghana, as a priority
step, but I have seen no reports on the output.
This is clearly an emergency measure. In my
judgment, these countries might better concentrate
on traditional undergraduate professions, such as
engineering, architecture, and economics, in which
a planning and development component will naturally
be very large.

WESTERN MODELS

Next, I would like to consider the changes that
might be made in the educational system, and
particularly in professional education, to render
it more relevant and more efficient from the stand-
point of the developing countries. My first principle
here is that professional education should be conducted primarily in the developing countries. There
it has the advantage that it is conducted under the
real conditions with which the profession must deal.
The social and professional challenges of the
developing area are apparent everywhere. The
conditions under which the future professional must
practice are available for study. The student will
not be misguided or confused by the irrelevant

standards of the West, which typically have little
applicability in developing countries. Finally, the
student is not exposed to the potentially seductive
standards of life and professional practice that
abound in Western countries.

There is nothing new in all of this. There
have been scores of efforts to establish new
institutions in the developing countries, particularly
the so-called regional institutions. Each of these
efforts has encountered familiar obstacles. It is
difficult and expensive to recruit faculty for many
areas. There are serious problems of turnover and
of acculturation of faculty drawn from the West,
and so on. However, if we keep in mind an attrition
rate of 50-80 per cent and accept the fact that
Western education may serve primarily to draw off
the most talented youth from the developing countries,
I think, in the long run, we will accept these higher
costs, face the problems, pay the price. This means
that we must reorient our common Western governmental
attitude that, somehow, these jobs can be done
quickly or cheaply. We must recognize that we will
be in business for at least a generation and must
prepare ourselves and our graduate students who are
interested in the developing countries for such
long-range missions.

A further major obstacle to training in the
developing countries is the prestige of the Western
degree. We should frankly recognize that in many
countries Western education commands such a premium
in the market that the local degree is simply not
competitive. Here again, however, we can be
inventive and devise ways of meeting the problem
frontally. We must induce our Western educational
institutions to establish campuses in the developing
countries, presumably on the existing campuses of
native institutions to facilitate recruitment. We
must persuade our Western institutions to grant
degrees for credits received in these foreign
campuses or centers so that the prestige of the
Western degree can accompany a training program
meeting Western standards. We can devise examining
procedures to assure that quality standards are
maintained. We can institute short-term visits to
the Western countries and their campuses to provide
whatever advantages accrue from foreign travel or
acquaintance with a wider range of professors and
graduate students of these degree-granting

institutions. A host of administrative devices
could be developed to overcome the psychological
and cultural disadvantages of concentrated training
in the developed countries.

Can we duplicate in the developing countries
the spirit of social and professional dedication which
we expect to be part of the climate in Western educational institutions? One of the important responsibilities is to provide the student with the motivation
and commitment to professional and scientific standards
which we expect from faculty and students alike.
Again, I believe that where such a spirit does not
already exist, it can be created by a sufficiently
dedicated faculty, a sufficiently selective admissions
policy, and perhaps by the use of campuses in the
developing countries for the terminal training of
particularly highly motivated Western students who
might serve as exemplars for their developing-area
peers where new or different motivation seems
desirable.

In some countries, there is another problem:
the insulation of the university from society.
American universities, in particular, draw heavily
upon the tradition of agricultural research and
extension, which commit educational institutions to
the service of society in research, in training, and
in certain forms of community leadership and action.
Most developing countries lack these traditions.
In many developing countries, however, we see the
emergence of research institutes connected with
universities whose purpose is to serve government
agencies or society. They are creating a link
between educational institutions and the surrounding
community. Where they are needed, it seems to me
that we can readily create such links and, through
the services that they render and the opportunities
for professional education that they provide, create
the linkages between research, training, and service
that appear necessary.

ALTERNATIVES

Formal educational institutions are not the
only means, nor necessarily the best, for professional education. Indeed, David Crane long ago
suggested that apprenticeship in a professional
office might be a more efficient device under
certain circumstances. In the evolution of Western

countries, apprenticeships, the architect's studio, reading for the law, and other forms of in-service training invariably preceded the establishment of formal educational institutions. In almost all of the professions, internship or other professional experience is required prior to licensing or other recognition of full professional status.

We can conceive of many devices through which the educational role of professional offices might be expanded. Suppose every planning contract carried a stipulation that every Western professional must assume responsibility for one counterpart professional trainee. I expect that the efficiency of the Western professional would be enhanced rather than reduced. His time lost in advice to the apprentice would be regained by the service the apprentice would render and the insights he could contribute. If every man year of Western professional time produced a man year of such educational time, we would have gained quite a bit. In addition, we would have identified those apprentices of extraordinary ability and dedication who would benefit most from further formal training.

The use of apprenticeship on a widespread basis has a further and secondary advantage. Those selected for training abroad after their period of apprenticeship could be provided an assured position upon return, which would be a very considerable incentive to return.

Further extending this idea, one wonders whether we would not be better off to recruit any trainees abroad not from the educational institutions so much as from government agencies and professional offices, where we might, presumably, be dealing with more seasoned students, perhaps more socially dedicated, and, quite possibly, ones who would be assured professional positions as an incentive for return.

Apprenticeship, however, will remain a fairly costly way of training a necessarily limited number of people. Could we not put apprenticeship on a mass production basis by some combination of in-service or extension training? The Ford-Calcutta project had this potential. A fairly modest staff of Western specialists was there, engaged in helping the native staff to develop a plan--essentially educating them regarding the tasks and methods thought to be relevant. It will be of interest to learn whether the participants believe there has been an educational

by-product. If so, we might explore other means for
in-service training and expand these from advisory
to advisory-educational ventures wherever a technical
assistance program is mounted. Technical assistance
could become a mode of in-service training, in which
the secondary objectives of training may be as
important as the primary function. Could we make
this process more efficient by providing correspon-
dence school types of teaching materials similar to
those developed by various armed services for the
training of soldiers for future civilian activity?
I still have the curriculum and texts that were
developed in Britain to train future planners during
World War II. They must have been of value to that
country after the war. Could we experiment by
providing several technical assistance missions with
such teaching materials?

There have been several proposals also for
traveling faculties or training centers. Under one
of these proposals, for instance, a faculty of five
members would be assembled for one year to offer a
three-month program in each of four countries. With
teaching materials prepared in advance, such a
faculty could offer intensive, short-term training
to a group already in school or on the job. It could
confer a foreign certificate. The recruitment
problems would be quite manageable.

INDUCEMENTS TO CHANGE

We must recognize that the educational system
has some responsibility for changing the environment
in which the professions have to work to make it more
attractive for the individual and to enhance the
influence of the professional in the developing
society. In the West, schools exercise a considerable influence on the professions. They redefine
the problems with which the professions must deal.
They continually influence the methods that each
profession uses, and they direct the stream of
graduates to those offices and agencies where
opportunities are greatest. One wonders whether
these influences might not be systematically
organized to put pressure on the surrounding
professional environment. If Western-supported
educational institutions conceive this to be part of
their mission, I am sure the influence would vary
widely from country to country and from profession
to profession. Doubtless, there have been instances

that could be studied. Doubtless, we could find the
tactics and policies that were most effective in
creating a challenging and rewarding environment
for work. Let me suggest a few.

Competitive opportunities for employment may
be a primary point of leverage upon existing
institutions. If our corps of trainees can readily
move into government, industry, research organizations,
or educational institutions, the competition among
these may enhance the influence of the professions
and raise their salaries. A program to set up new
institutions to provide such competitive outlets for
skilled people becomes a part of a broad development
program. We have mentioned professional offices,
research units, development companies, consulting
firms, and we must remember international agencies.
The proliferation of successful agencies in almost
any field might help.

The creation of an elite corps of public
servants is not a new problem. The British and
Indian Administration Class and others systematically rotate the assignments of their younger
members, especially in the early years, to provide
them with a wide range of experiences, varying
types and levels of work, and exposure to a multitude
of experiences. Each country could initiate such a
corps, but on a wider basis, rotating the members
not only within central government but in state or
local, in private industry, educational institutions,
and United Nations or other international agencies.
Essential in such a system is cumulative experience,
which puts high demands upon the individual, and
rapidly increasing responsibility. After such an
experience, people will be impatient of unnecessary
delay, ready to move from unpromising situations,
more able to take risks and make difficult decisions.

What other conditions can we create which will
enhance personal success, provide assurance of
professional competence, and provide the willingness
to lead? Salaries need improvement, of course, but
can we not reach further? I've often wondered what
would happen if we provided each of our returning
graduates with $100,000 in equity capital and
suggested that he go into the home-building business
on the side. I can't believe that we wouldn't have
today a dozen millionaires in a dozen countries,
each swinging a lot of political weight in his
native country, each a powerful force for the better

organization of development activity. More
important, the opportunity might spur government
agencies to more vigorous action, to providing
greater opportunity for their young professionals.

There are other devices to confer status and
influence for achievement. National and international professional societies, and other systems
of recognition, both confer status on the individual
and provide him with a broader acquaintance, broader
knowledge, and potential mobility. Field by field,
we might consider the marginal value of expenditures
for these purposes. This enumeration is incomplete,
but it does attempt to suggest means beyond ordinary
professional training that would radically enhance
the efficiency of training efforts.

RELATING SUPPLY TO DEMAND:
THE IMPORTANCE OF DIVERSITY

It will be impossible to deal with curriculum
content in this form. Some years ago, Harvey Perloff
set forth his views on this subject, and that work
continues to have much urgency. I should note,
however, that the quantitative requirements vary
widely by level and field of training. We need a
few very broad and scholarly planners with comprehensive training. We need thousands of specialists
capable of directing action at the city or project
level. We need a few national or regional economists
highly skilled in development economies. We need
thousands who can work on a housing project or the
financing of a utility system. We need a modest
corps of teachers at the Ph.D. level. We need
thousands of front-line practitioners at the level
of the first professional degree.

Reference has already been made to the broad
range of subject matter specialists require. Most
important are general public administrators,
especially for local government, and generalist
local physical planners, who, presumably, must also
be architects or engineers. The development
coordinator has evolved in the United States as
one who has the skills of a public administrator
as well as those of a private real estate developer--
we need many in this field. Architects and engineers
with supplementary training in economics and administration are needed at every level. From several
disciplines we should train people for economic

analysis and development programing at the metropolitan level. Finally, public health administration is
a prestigious and important field everywhere. In the
long run, our needs for people in business administration, banking, mortgage lending, and construction may
equal or exceed needs in the public sector.

This enumeration largely neglects planning for
social services, in part because it has been confined,
to date, to health and education, to the neglect of
broader and more comprehensive planning. The field
is new; in the future, it must become far more
important.

THE NEED FOR A MULTILEVEL APPROACH

In the nineteenth century, development proceeded
very largely from the bottom up. The market and
local services served and central government only
provided a framework of law, though that was fundamental to the creation of conditions for growth.
In the twentieth century, we have had extensive
experience, particularly in the U.S.S.R., with
development directed from the top down. That system
has not achieved much higher rates of development.
It is certainly debatable whether, on balance, it
has made the process more humane, more equitable,
or more stable. If one can make a sweeping generalization, it would be that development is fostered best
by circumstances in which both centrally directed and
grass roots-motivated development are proceeding at
approximately the same pace. Then, local expectations
will not exceed realizable possibilities, and central
directives or incentives will not fail for lack of
local implementation.

If this is a reasonable hypothesis, then it
should be a basic guide to educational policy for
development. We need to attend to basic popular
education. In professional education, we should
direct our efforts toward a large number of people
who will work at the local level, in government,
business, and nonprofit institutions. But,
particularly at the local level, we must deal with
the problems of popular cultural transformation.
This is work for religious leaders, political
leaders, those who preside over television, the
press, and other communication, and those who deal
with the symbols and rites that give life meaning
and order. We are not yet ready, I hope, to train

a breed of cultural factors engineers, but we must
do something to instill in our development planners
a profound sensitivity to these forces. The humani-
zation of development planning is as essential as its
efficiency. Indeed, that political stability which
is a prerequisite to success may depend, in large
degree, upon our sensitivity to the humane and
cultural issues in development. Here, then, is a
field in which our knowledge is discouragingly
limited and the challenges enormous.

NOTE TO CHAPTER 5

1. Charles Susskind, "A Study of Foreign
Students Who Received Graduate Engineering Degrees
at Berkeley, 1954-1965" (Berkeley: University of
California, 1967).

DATE DUE